LANGUAGE TOOLKIT

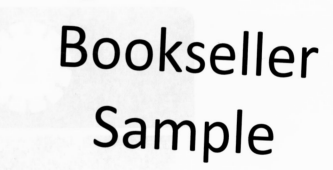

FOR THE AUSTRALIAN CURRICULUM

Second edition

ANDREA HAYES

CAMBRIDGE
UNIVERSITY PRESS

CAMBRIDGE
UNIVERSITY PRESS

477 Williamstown Road, Port Melbourne, VIC 3207, Australia

Cambridge University Press is part of the University of Cambridge.

It furthers the University's mission by disseminating knowledge in the pursuit of education, learning and research at the highest international levels of excellence.

www.cambridge.edu.au
Information on this title: www.cambridge.org/9781107697928

First published 2010
Reprinted 2011
Second edition 2014

Cover designed by Luke Harris
Typeset by Sylvia Witte
Printed in China by C&C Offset Printing Co. Ltd.

ISBN 978-1-107-69792-8 Paperback

Additional resources for this publication at www.cambridge.edu.au/GO

TABLE OF CONTENTS

ABOUT THE AUTHOR

Andrea Hayes is an English teacher, freelance writer and English consultant. She currently teaches English at Brighton Grammar School and regularly delivers workshops for English teachers. Andrea has written numerous textbooks, magazine articles and education resources – print, blended and online. A teacher with over 25 years of experience, Andrea has also worked as an education and English consultant for Screen Australia, Video Education and the Australian Television Foundation.

AUTHOR ACKNOWLEDGEMENTS

Andrea Hayes would like to thank the following people for their support and contributions: Colin Chen, Gus Jahn and Lucas Cheesman for their short story examples, Timothy Semmens for his film review, the English students and staff at Brighton Grammar School, Kris Patterson for her book advice, Luisa Catalano, Jennifer Blackburn, Rosanna Fimiani, Rose Larkin, Martin Hayes and John Catalano.

PUBLISHER'S ACKNOWLEDGEMENTS

The author and publisher wish to thank the following sources for permission to reproduce material:

Images: 2014 Used under license from Shutterstock.com / Cathy Keifer, **p.2** / Sashkin, **p.4** / Everett Collection, **p.7** / PeJo, **p.9** / Photo Works, **p.13** / solarseven, **p.17** / Kae Deezign, **p.20** / Suzanne Tucker, **p.28** / Sergemi, **p.31** / Arena Photo UK, **p.33** / Halfpoint, **p.39** / hempuli, **p.40** / Aleph Studio, **p.42** / Kozoriz Yuriy, **p.44** / Tomnamon, **p.49** / Sofiaworld, **p.53** / Cathy Brinkworth, **p.60** / Lance Bellers, **p.66** / Yuriy Vlasenko, **p.77** / IvicaNS, **p.79** / Jag_cz, **p.86** / RazoomGame, **p.93** / Roxana Gonzalez, **p.95** / Chantal de Bruijne, **p.97** / siouxsinner, **p.100** / Berents, **p.110** / Triff, **p.114** / Lobke Peers, **p.121(l)** / Maxim Blinkov, **p.121(r)** / Christian Mueller, **p.122(l)** / Ozerov Alexander, **p.122(r)** / Ivonne Wierink, **p.136** / cosma, **p.139** / Melkor3D, **p.147** / Africa Studio, **p.152** / Blend Images, **p.164** / Rena Schild, **p.165** / Stuart Miles, **p.179** / YuryImaging, **p.189** / V.J. Matthew, **p.191** / Alexandra Thompson, **p.202** / Lance Bellers, **p.206** / Robbie Taylor, **p.207** / Igor Bulgarin, **p.211**; Images from *The Arrival* by Shaun Tan, Lothian Children's Books, an imprint of Hachette Australia, 2006, reprinted by permission, **p.124**.

Text: "Man tries to smuggle 43 lizards in underwear", *The Daily Telegraph*, 9 December 2009, **p.2**; From *Never Mind the Bullocks, Here's the Science* by Dr. Karl Kruszelnicki, reprinted by permission of HarperCollins Publishers, **p.17**; From *The Outsiders* by S.E. Hinton (Victor Gollancz, 1970). Copyright © S.E. Hinton, 1967. Reproduced by permission of Penguin Books Ltd, UK. Reproduced digitally by permission of Curtis Brown, Ltd, **p.28**; © Gemma Malley, 2007, *The Declaration*, Bloomsbury Publishing Plc, **p.53**; From *The Rage of Sheep* by Michelle Cooper. Copyright © Michelle Cooper 2007. Reprinted by permission of Random House Australia, **p.95**; "Mushrooms" in *Collected Poems* by Sylvia Plath. Reproduced by permission of Faber and Faber Ltd, **p.110**; From *Wonder* by R.J. Palacio. Published by Random House Children's Books. Reprinted by permission of the The Random House Group Limited, **p.179**; From *A Bridge to Wiseman's Cove* by James Maloney (UQP 1996). Reprinted by permission of University of Queensland Press, **p.191**; Copyright © 2009 Tony Thompson. Extract from *Shakespeare: the most famous man in London*. Reproduced by permission of Walker Books Australia, **p.206**.

Every effort has been made to trace and acknowledge copyright. The publisher apologises for any accidental infringement and welcomes information that would redress this situation.

INTRODUCTION

Dear student,

Language Toolkit 2 for the Australian Curriculum is a language workbook for middle secondary students based on the Australian Curriculum. It contains 16 units arranged around different texts. For your teacher's easy reference, the front page of each unit lists the modes, cross-curriculum priorities, general capabilities and content from the Australian Curriculum covered in the unit.

Each unit is organised into six sections:

Reading tools – comprehension style questions on a text

Grammar tools – grammar rule with clear examples and exercises

Vocabulary tools – rules and guidelines followed by exercises that develop vocabulary skills

Editing tools – spelling and punctuation rules and exercises designed to help you avoid common errors and improve your writing skills

Writing and creating tools – tasks that draw together skills learnt in a unit including crafted pieces of writing plus options to rework these pieces into multimodal texts and/or oral presentations.

Language Toolkit 2 for the Australian Curriculum also contains four sets of Revision Tools. These are quick quizzes that help you review your progress.

If you are lucky your teacher may allow you to complete units in class or even as homework!

Please remember:

- if you want to record, photograph or upload video of friends or family you need to ask their permission first, especially if you are placing them on Youtube or Instagram
- avoid using pirated or illegally downloaded films or soundtracks when completing creative tasks
- follow copyright regulations, cite sources and do not pretend that someone else's work is your own (plagiarise).

Have fun and learn lots!

Andrea Hayes
Author

Dear teacher,

Please note that answers to questions in *Language Toolkit 2 for the Australian Curriculum* (except for the activities in the Writing and Creating Tools sections) are available on the *Cambridge GO* website.

Andrea Hayes

LANGUAGE
TOOLKIT

2

Unit 1

Information texts: Online newspaper article

Tools in this unit

- Reading tools: Understanding 'Man tries to smuggle 43 lizards in underwear'
- Grammar tools: Nouns
- Vocabulary tools: Syllables
- Spelling tools: Singular and plural nouns
- Punctuation tools: Capital letters and full stops
- Writing and creating tools: Write an online news article

Modes covered

- Receptive: Reading and listening
- Productive: Writing, speaking and creating

General capabilities

- Literacy
- Information and communication technology capability
- Critical and creative thinking

Curriculum content in this unit

- Text structure and organisation: ACELA1543, ACELA1766, ACELA1544
- Expressing and developing ideas: ACELA1545, ACELA1549
- Examining literature: ACELT1630, ACELT1767
- Texts in context: ACELY1729
- Interacting with others: ACELY1808, ACELY1731
- Interpreting, analysing, evaluating: ACELY1732, ACELY1734
- Creating texts: ACELY1736, ACELY1738

Man tries to smuggle 43 lizards in underwear

A German visitor was caught trying to leave New Zealand with 23 geckos and 20 skinks hidden in his underwear, a court was told.

Hans Kubus, 58, was stopped at Christchurch Airport on Sunday after checking in and was searched by customs staff.

A small package containing the reptiles was found in his underwear, prosecutor Mike Bodie told the Christchurch District Court yesterday.

'The package contained eight separate compartments separating various gecko and skink species,' he said.

Kubus' luggage also contained a single gecko in a rolled-up sock.

A total of 23 geckos were found from five different species, as well as 20 skinks from two species.

The German admitted trading geckos and taking geckos and skinks from the wild without a permit.

A black market trade in geckos exists in Europe and those taken by Kubus would have had a street value of around $NZ50 000 ($39 000), Mr Bodie said.

The value of the skinks was unknown because trading in that species had not previously been identified.

Kubus was due to be sentenced on January 25.

Source: *The Daily Telegraph*, 9 December 2009

Understanding 'Man tries to smuggle 43 lizards in underwear'

Read **'Man tries to smuggle 43 lizards in underwear'** then answer the following questions. You may use a dictionary.

1 Which country is Hans Kubus from?

....

2 Where were the reptiles hidden?

....

3 Who is Mike Bodie?

....

4 How many different species were there altogether?

....

5 What does the phrase 'black market trade' mean?

....

....

6 Which of the following questions have been answered in the first paragraph? Tick one box only.

Who? ❑

What? ❑

When? ❑

Where? ❑

Why? ❑

7 List the four types of information given using numbers.

----

8 In what way are the words in the first paragraph written differently from the rest of the article?

----

9 What is the source (publication and date) of the article?

----

10 Describe the action to be taken against Kubus.

Nouns

Nouns are naming words. They name people, places, animals, things, qualities, emotions and conditions; for example, Bruce, Australia, kangaroo, football, determination.

There are four types of nouns:

1 **Proper nouns** begin with a capital letter and name people, places, titles, days and months.

Examples: Port Douglas, Henry, the Pope, Wednesday, October

2 **Common nouns** name general things around you that you can see and touch.

Examples: table, cat, tree, cake, banana

3 **Collective nouns** name groups or collections of people, animals and things.

Examples: choir, team, herd

4 **Abstract nouns** name things you can't see, touch or measure, such as emotions, qualities and conditions.

Examples: love, fear, sadness, reliability

1 Locate the six nouns in the first paragraph of the article and write them below.

....

....

2 List the five common nouns in the first paragraph.

....

....

3 List the two proper nouns in the last paragraph.

....

....

4 Classify the following nouns by writing their type next to each one.

a compartments ....

b Brian ....

c package..

d luggage ....

e permit ....

f staff ....

5 Write the correct collective nouns from the box for the following.

smack	rafter	crash	parliament	pride	murder

a group of owls ....

b group of crows ....

c group of lions ....

d group of jellyfish ....

e group of pigeons ....

f group of rhinoceroses ....

6 A **shatner** is a new collective noun for a group of nerds. It comes from the surname of the actor, William Shatner (pictured opposite), who played Captain Kirk in the original *Star Trek* TV series.

Make up your own collective nouns for the following groups of things.

a group of wailing cats ....

b group of devoted football fans ....

c leftover vegetables on a plate ....

d group of older actors in a film ....

e group of chairs ....

f group of broken toys ....

7 List as many common nouns as alternatives for product (for hair) as you can in 60 seconds.

8 Circle the three abstract nouns in the box below that describe Hans Kubus' experience.

fear   happiness   anger   joy   anxiety   patience

Vocabulary tools

Syllables

Syllables are the separate sounds that make up a word. When you break a word into separate syllables it is easier to pronounce and spell. Syllables consist of a vowel sound with or without one or more consonant sounds.

For example, the word 'syllable' contains three syllables: **syll / a / ble**.

Things to note:

- Words that have only one syllable are called 'monosyllabic'.

- When two vowels are next to each other but give only one vowel sound, they count as one syllable.

Examples: great, slee / ping

- Sometimes the letter 'y' acts as a vowel.

Examples: sky, ci / ty

- An easy way to separate the sounds is to tap the beat as you sound the word.

1   Divide the following **common nouns** into syllables using a forward slash. Here's an example to show you how it's done:

reptiles = rep / tiles

a   gecko _____

b   admitted _____

c   underwear _____

d   smuggle _____

e   separate _____

f   identified _____

g compartments ....

h prosecutor ....

2 List three **monosyllabic** words you know.

....

....

3 Write your full name and divide it into syllables.

....

Spelling tools

Singular and plural nouns

Singular nouns name a person, place, creature, emotion or thing. *Examples:* city, canary, crowd, illness

Plural nouns name more than one. *Examples:* cities, canaries, crowds, illnesses

Five rules for spelling plural nouns

1 Add 's' to a singular noun.

Examples: dog – dogs ➡ chair – chairs

2 When a noun ends in 's', 'sh', 'ch', 'x' or 'ss' add the ending 'es'.

Examples: box – boxes ➡ crash – crashes ➡ patch – patches ➡ kiss – kisses

3 For most nouns that end in 'o' add the ending 'es'.

Examples: potato – potatoes ➡ tomato – tomatoes

Exception: video – videos

4 When a noun ends in 'y' and there is a consonant immediately before 'y' you must change 'y' to 'i' and add 'es'.

Examples: hobby – hobbies ➡ lolly – lollies

5 For most nouns that end in 'f' change the 'f' to 'v', then add 'es'.

Examples: loaf – loaves ➡ leaf – leaves

Exceptions: reef – reefs ➡ roof – roofs

Fix it!

Some plural nouns do not follow any of these rules.
You'll be introduced to these in Unit 2.

1 Change the following singular nouns into their plural forms.

a sock ....

b match ....

c gecko ....

d tomato ....

e fox ....

f country ....

2 Underline the 10 spelling mistakes in the following text. Write the words correctly in the space provided.

I read an article once about a guy who kept calfs, wolfs (OK, maybe they were dingos) and doges INSIDE his house in the cities! Apparently he fed them potatos and loafs of bread and they were not house trained. One days, two thiefs broke into his place to steal his TV and other important stuff. They were so grossed out by the smell that they ran for their life!

....

....

Capital letters and full stops

Five rules for capital letters

1 Proper nouns must begin with a capital letter.

Example: Michael is my friend from Sydney.

2 The first word of every sentence must begin with a capital letter.

Example: The pies at my local bakery are delicious.

3 'I' is always written using a capital letter.

Example: When I play the piano I feel a sense of satisfaction.

4 A capital letter must be used at the beginning of words spoken, even when they follow a comma.

Example: Luke asked, 'Where is my blanket?'

5 Capital letters are used at the start of every main word in the title of a film, book or play and in the name of a person or a place.

Example: The Lizards are in my Underwear.

Full stops

A full stop must be used at the end of every sentence that is not a question or an exclamation.

Fix it!

Not all company names, advertisements and film, CD, book and magazine titles use correct capitalisation. Sometimes new designs and styles use lower case for effect.

Example: sanderson solicitors & co.

1 Edit the following conversation by adding eight full stops and sixteen capital letters.

Carlos said, 'i don't understand how a person can fit so many lizards in their undies'

'wouldn't they bite?' asked maree

'i think the guy from germany drugged them!' said tim

'why do you think the customs staff at christchurch searched him?' inquired maree

'maybe he was walking funny the package had eight compartments,' suggested carlos

'must have been a giant pair of undies,' said tim

carlos and maree nodded

2 Rewrite the following titles adding capital letters.

a 'dr who and the giant lizards'

....

b 'australian celebrity lizards masterchef'

....

c 'bend it like beckham's lizards'

....

Writing and creating tools

Good writers take the following essential steps:

- **Research** and **plan** before they start to write.

- **Draft**, **edit** and **proofread** before finalising their work.

Good writers also carefully 'map' out their writing by asking and answering the following questions:

- **Message – what** the main point is that you want to tell your readers; e.g. dogs are a lot of fun.

- **Audience – who** will read your piece; e.g. dad, lizard owners, neighbours.

- **Purpose – why** you are writing this piece; e.g. to describe, to instruct, to persuade, to imagine.

- **Style – how** your piece will look and sound; e.g. funny, friendly, angry, an article, formal or informal language.

Writing task

Write an article for an online newspaper using one of the headlines in the following box. Your article should be 150 words and should include one-sentence paragraphs.

Dog found in aeroplane luggage!	Woman caught with rare birds!
Drug bust!	Stolen phones found in school bag!
Suspicious package found!	Your own headline

1 **Research** – Choose your headline and write notes to answer the following: Who? What? Where? When? Why?

2 **Plan** – Consider the following for your article: the message of your article, your intended audience, the purpose of your article and the style in which you will write it.

3 **Draft** – Draft your article under the following headings:

- Paragraph 1 (Who? What? Where?)

....

- Paragraph 2 (When? More details)

....

- Paragraph 3 (More details about the item found)

....

- Paragraph 4 (Suggest reasons why)

....

- Paragraph 5 (What action is taken?)

....

4 **Edit and proofread** – Check spelling, punctuation and word limit. Have you used capital letters and full stops correctly? Read over what you have written – is your article interesting and does it make sense?

Creating task

Explore **multimodal presentation methods** for your online newspaper article.

- Using PowerPoint, create a visual storyboard of your article that incorporates images and words.

- Start a class **Wiki** for everyone's news articles. You or your classmates may wish to add to it every week with important news about people in your class.

Listen and respond to what other students have done.

- Deliver your finished article as a three-minute **oral presentation** – in pairs or small groups.

- Write a 50-word summary of the presentations you have heard. Include comments about the **purpose** and **audience** of these presentations.

- Describe the language used in each presentation and online newspaper article. Does it sound (tone) serious or amusing? What words make it sound this way?

Unit

Information texts: Non-fiction

Tools in this unit

- Reading tools: Understanding 'Vomit Comet' and 'There ain't no zero'
- Grammar tools: Nouns – gender
- Vocabulary tools: Using a dictionary
- Spelling tools: Plural nouns – three exceptions
- Punctuation tools: Quotation marks
- Writing and creating tools: Write a factual information text

Modes covered

- Receptive: Reading and listening
- Productive: Speaking, writing and creating

General capabilities

- Literacy
- Information and communication technology capability
- Critical and creative thinking

Curriculum content in this unit

- Language for interaction: ACELA1541
- Text structure and organisation: ACELA1766, ACELA1809, ACELA1544
- Expressing and developing ideas: ACELA1547, ACELA1549
- Responding to literature: ACELT1628, ACELT1807
- Texts in context: ACELY1729
- Interacting with others: ACELY1730, ACELY1808, ACELY1731
- Interpreting, analysing, evaluating: ACELY1732, ACELY1733, ACELY1734
- Creating texts: ACELY1736, ACELY1810, ACELY1738

Responding to texts

Never Mind the Bullocks, Here's the Science by Karl Kruszelnicki (2009)

Vomit Comet

The 'Vomit Comet' was the name given to the aeroplanes operated by the NASA Reduced Gravity Research Foundation. By flying in a series of up-and-down curves, each about 10 km long, the pilots can generate about 25 seconds of effective weightlessness for every 65 seconds of flight. Of course, there's no such thing as a free lunch, so the 25 seconds of weightlessness are balanced by a similar period of double gravity.

The name Vomit Comet arose because, under these trying conditions, about one-third of passengers vomited a lot, about one-third were just nauseated and felt like vomiting, and about one-third were unaffected.

The first NASA Vomit Comet was a Lockheed C-131. After its retirement from service in 1959, it was replaced by two KC-135 Stratotankers. One, NASA 930, was used to film weightlessness sequences for the movie *Apollo 13* . . .

In 2005, NASA began using a C-9B Skytrain II. And NASA renamed it with the 'nicer' nickname of 'Weightless Wonder' rather than 'Vomit Comet'. (p. 132)

There ain't no zero

The astronauts in orbit are not in 'zero gravity'.

Nope, the gravity of every object (no matter how little mass it has) reaches to the very edges of the Universe.

The gravitational field becomes weaker as it gets further away, but it never drops to zero. (p. 126)

Source: Kruszelnicki, K. 2009, *Never Mind the Bullocks, Here's the Science*, HarperCollins Publishers, Australia.

Understanding 'Vomit Comet' and 'There ain't no zero'

Read the extracts 'Vomit Comet' and 'There ain't no zero', then answer the following questions. You may use a dictionary.

1 What type of machine was the Vomit Comet? How did it get its nickname?

....

....

....

2 What happened in 1959?

....

....

....

3 Why was NASA 930 famous?

....

4 What does the title 'There ain't no zero' refer to?

....

....

5 Tick one box only to answer each of the following questions:

a Which best describes the purpose of this text?

to amuse ☐   to explain ☐   to persuade ☐

b Which word best describes the information contained in the two extracts?

fiction ☐   fact ☐   myth ☐

c Who is the intended audience for these extracts?

astronauts ☐   tourists ☐   science enthusiasts ☐

6 What does 'nauseated' mean?

....

7 What film is mentioned in the extract?

....

⚒ Grammar tools

Nouns – gender

Nouns name people, places, animals, things, qualities, emotions and conditions. The **gender** of a noun refers to whether it is masculine (male) or feminine (female). An example of a masculine noun is **uncle**; an example of a feminine noun is **Diana**.

If a noun has no gender it is described as **neuter**. *Example:* bicycle

Some nouns can be both masculine and feminine. *Examples:* politician, actor

1 Classify the following nouns according to their gender by adding them to the correct column in the table below.

man	tree	woman	pen	manager	pilot	aeroplane	poet
lioness	niece	bachelor	enemy	relative	hen	stallion	
sow	school	singer	heir	Alex	widow	sir	Maggie

Masculine	Feminine	Masculine and feminine	Neuter

2 Complete the following sentences by adding the correct nouns.

a The son of a king is called a _____.

b The owner of a hotel is called a _____.

c The wife of a duke is called a _____.

d The father of my husband is called my _____.

Vocabulary tools

Using a dictionary

Five things you should know about dictionaries

1 A dictionary is an essential tool for all English students.

2 Dictionaries can be online or printed; e.g. http://dictionary.reference.com is the website of an online dictionary.

3 Dictionaries (print only) are permitted in most English exams.

4 Dictionaries help you to find:

- correct spellings of words

- new words

- parts of speech; e.g. noun, verb

- origins of words.

5 Some printed dictionaries have added extras such as lists of abbreviations, common words, spelling rules or lists of synonyms.

1 Use a dictionary and write brief definitions for the following words. You can use either a printed or an online dictionary.

a gravity

....

b weightlessness

....

c nauseated

....

d orbit

....

....

2 Use each of the following words in a sentence to show its meaning.

patriotism   juggernaut   catastrophe   incandescent

....

....

....

....

....

....

....

....

Plural nouns – three exceptions

Unit 1 contains five rules for spelling plural nouns (see p. 10). There are some exceptions to these rules:

1 Nouns with the same spelling for singular and plural

Examples: salmon, deer, trout, sheep, swine

2 Nouns that have totally different singular and plural forms

Examples: foot – feet; tooth – teeth; datum – data; ox – oxen; medium – media; criterion – criteria

3 Nouns that have no singular form

Examples: measles, trousers, tweezers, sunglasses, thanks, tongs

1 Use a dictionary and write the plural form of the following singular nouns.

a hoof ....

b knife ....

c box ....

d loaf ....

2 Underline the incorrect nouns in 'Space story' and write the correct versions of the nouns in the space provided.

Space story

An astronauts flew out of Earth's orbits to another planets in the Universes. On that planet lived a very different specie. They were very tall aliens with three foots and huge rotten tooths. The astronaut used his tweezer and took sample of alien skins. It was full of puses! Yeuww!! Revolting!

Quotation marks

Quotation marks are also called talking marks or inverted commas. They can be single (' ') or double (" ").

Four rules for quotation marks

1 Quotation marks are used for **titles** of poems, short stories and newspaper articles, as well as titles of books and films when you handwrite an essay.

Example: One of the most well known poems by John Keats is called 'Ode to a Nightingale'.

However, it is more appropriate for the titles of books, plays and films to be italicised.

Example: The Boy in the Striped Pyjamas, The Arrival, The Outsiders, Romeo and Juliet

2 Sometimes quotation marks are used to indicate that a particular word or phrase may have an unexpected meaning.

Example: I could have done without all his 'helpful' suggestions.

3 Place quotation marks at the start and end of actual words spoken (**direct speech**) and outside other punctuation marks if these are part of the quotation.

Example: 'I feel sick,' complained Riley.

4 If direct speech includes a quotation, use single quotation marks to show the **direct speech** and double quotation marks to show the quotation within the direct speech.

Example: 'I heard a boy say "I'm lost" at the train station,' reported Kathryn.

1 List the four words or terms singled out with quotation marks in 'Vomit Comet' and 'There ain't no zero'.

----

2 Rewrite the following sentences, adding quotation marks where needed.

a I've also read Please Explain and Bumbreath, Botox and Bubbles, which are two other books by Dr Karl.

b I would be so sick if I had flown in the Vomit Comet, remarked Sian.

c If you yelled, help in space, who would hear you? asked Tran.

d Ted wondered, If you are weightless, does your vomit float?

Writing and creating tools

Writing task

Write an information text that explains one of the topics in the box. Your explanation should be 150–200 words and include the following:

- facts
- a list of your sources
- a visual (graph, chart or diagram) if necessary.

Topics:

a new machine or vehicle	a famous invention	a famous discovery
a scientific breakthrough	an amazing plant	a topic of your choice

1 **Research** – Research your topic (using your library or the internet). Organise your notes under the following headings: facts, important dates, impact on people. Record your sources in alphabetical order.

2 **Plan** – Number your notes in the order that you will write them.

3 **Draft** – Write your information text and list your sources of information at the end.

4 **Edit and proofread** – Check that you have used quotation marks correctly. Check spelling and other punctuation. Read over your explanation. Have you provided a clear explanation of your topic?

Creating task

Explore **multimodal presentation methods** for your information text.

- Present your information text as a brochure or poster, either hand drawn or in digital format. Make sure you include visuals, either diagrams or pictures.

Listen and respond to what other students have done.

- Deliver your text as an **oral presentation** that incorporates a strong visual element; e.g. a photograph or diagram.

- Write a 50-word summary of one of the presentations including comments on the following:

    - the order in which information is presented

    - a description of the language used

    - the impact the visual element has on the audience.

Unit

Literary texts: Descriptive writing

Tools in this unit

- Reading tools: Understanding *The Outsiders*
- Grammar tools: Adjectives
- Vocabulary tools: Using a thesaurus – synonyms and antonyms
- Spelling tools: Prefixes and suffixes
- Punctuation tools: Hyphens
- Writing and creating tools: Write a physical description

Modes covered

- Receptive: Reading, listening and viewing
- Productive: Speaking, writing and creating

General capabilities

- Literacy
- Personal and social capability
- Information and communication technology capability
- Critical and creative thinking
- Ethical understanding

Curriculum content in this unit

- Language for interaction: ACELA1541
- Text structure and organisation: ACELA1766, ACELA1809, ACELA1544
- Expressing and developing ideas: ACELA1547
- Literature and context: ACELT1626
- Responding to literature: ACELT1627, ACELT1807
- Examining literature: ACELT1629, ACELT1767
- Creating literature: ACELT1768
- Interacting with others: ACELY1808, ACELY1731
- Interpreting, analysing, evaluating: ACELY1732, ACELY1733, ACELY1735
- Creating texts: ACELY1736, ACELY1810, ACELY1738

Responding to texts

The Outsiders by S.E. Hinton (1967)

Anyway, I went on walking home, thinking about the movie, and then suddenly wishing I had some company. Greasers can't walk alone too much or they'll get jumped, or someone will come by and scream 'Greaser!' at them, which doesn't make you feel too hot, if you know what I mean. We get jumped by Socs. I'm not sure how you spell it, but it's the abbreviation for the Socials, the jet set, the West-side rich kids. It's like the term 'greaser,' which is used to class all us boys on the East Side.

We're poorer than the Socs and the middle class. I reckon we're wilder, too. Not like the Socs, who jump greasers and wreck houses and throw beer blasts for kicks, and get editorials in the paper for being a public disgrace one day and an asset to society the next. Greasers are almost like hoods; we steal things and

drive old souped-up cars and hold up gas stations and have a gang fight once in a while. I don't mean I do things like that. Darry would kill me if I got into trouble with the police. Since Mom and Dad were killed in an auto wreck, the three of us get to stay together only as long as we behave. So Soda and I stay out of trouble as much as we can, and we're careful not to get caught when we can't. I only mean that most greasers do things like that, just like we wear our hair long and dress in blue jeans and T-shirts, or leave our shirttails out and wear leather jackets and tennis shoes or boots. I'm not saying that either Socs or greasers are better; that's just the way things are.

Source: Hinton, S.E. 1967, *The Outsiders*, Penguin, London, p. 4.

Understanding *The Outsiders*

Read the extract from **The Outsiders**, then answer the following questions. You may use a dictionary.

1 Who are the two groups described in this extract?

....

2 List the three other names used to describe the 'Socials'.

....

3 List the four things greasers do.

....

....

4 What do you think the term 'hoods' means?

....

5 Tick one box only to answer each of the following questions:

a What type of text does this extract come from?

poem ❑   play ❑   novel ❑

b Who is telling or narrating the story?

a greaser ❑   a Soc ❑   Darry ❑

c Who do you think are the intended audience for this text?

criminals ❑   teachers ❑   teenagers ❑

d Which best describes the message of this text?

that life can be difficult for some teenagers   ❑

that poor kids are always criminals   ❑

that all rich kids waste their money   ❑

Grammar tools

Adjectives

Adjectives are **describing words**. Specifically, they **describe nouns and pronouns**, or people, places, things, feelings and experiences. Adjectives **tell us something more** about the **quality** of the noun or pronoun being used. Adjectives can help the reader to imagine the characters and places that you describe by creating pictures in their minds. For example, you might write a simple sentence like this:

There is a spider in my kitchen.

However, adding adjectives to your sentence to describe the nouns ('spider' and 'kitchen') helps to create a more vivid picture of what's going on.

There is a **big**, **hairy** spider in my **messy** kitchen.

1   Locate the adjectives in the extract and list them in the space below.

....

....

2   Referring to the extract again, write down the adjectives used to describe the following.

a   the 'blasts' the Socs have ....

b   the type of disgrace the Socs are ....

c   the cars the greasers drive ....

d   the type of fights the greasers have ....

3   In the following lists, three of the four adjectives mean nearly the same thing. Underline the word that doesn't fit. You can use a dictionary.

a   trouble   nuisance   simple   dilemma

b   nasty   caring   malevolent   spiteful

c   lonely   isolated   remote   connected

4 Use each of the following adjectives in a sentence with one additional adjective of your choice.

obnoxious   dangerous   reliable   generous

Vocabulary tools

Using a thesaurus – synonyms and antonyms

A thesaurus is a useful tool for writers and for helping you build your vocabulary skills.

A thesaurus lists **synonyms**, or different words that have identical or similar meanings.

Example: broke, deprived and destitute are all synonyms for poor.

Sometimes a thesaurus also includes different or opposite meanings. These are called **antonyms**.

Example: rich, privileged and loaded are all antonyms for poor.

Unlike a dictionary, a thesaurus does not include definitions of the word or the pronunciation of the word.

Some antonyms are formed using prefixes.

Example: helpful – unhelpful

Some antonyms are formed using suffixes.

Example: worthwhile – worthless

There are a number of print versions available, *Roget's Thesaurus* being the world's oldest; however, you can also access a thesaurus online, for example at http://thesaurus.com.

Note this:

A thesaurus is not usually permitted in a test or exam.

1 Using a thesaurus, write five synonyms each for the following over-used adjectives.

Over-used adjective	Synonyms
angry	
boring	
nice	
scared	
wonderful	

Spelling tools

Prefixes and suffixes

A **prefix** is a word or syllable placed at the beginning of a base word or root word to change its meaning.

A **suffix** is a word or syllable placed at the end of a base word to form a new word.

A **base word** is a word in its simplest form.

$$\underset{\text{base word}}{\underbrace{\overset{\text{prefix} \qquad \text{suffix}}{\text{disappearing}}}}$$

The following prefixes are known as **negative prefixes**, which all mean not:

	un	in	il	im	ir

Adding a negative prefix to the word **happy** changes its meaning to not happy.

Example: happy – unhappy

When you add the prefixes 'il', 'im' and 'ir' to adjectives that begin with 'l', 'm' and 'r', letters are doubled.

Examples: responsible – irresponsible, modest – immodest, logical – illogical

1 Change the following adjectives into their negative forms by adding the correct prefixes.

a animate _____

b religious _____

c cautious _____

d legal _____

e mortal _____

f affected _____

2 Write antonyms for the following words by adding one of the following prefixes: un, dis, in, im.

a possible ....

b conventional ....

c famous ....

d respect ....

3 Write antonyms for the following words by changing the suffixes.

a useless ....

b careless ....

c merciless ....

d cheerless ....

⚒ Punctuation tools

Hyphens

A hyphen is a punctuation tool that you use between words to help you avoid some common spelling problems.

1 Hyphens are used to join special prefixes to base words.

Examples: de-ice, self-control, re-enter, ill-treat

2 Hyphens are used to avoid confusion with word meanings.

Examples: resign compared to re-sign

Fix it!
Some commonly used words are no longer spelt with hyphens. These include 'thank you' and 'windowsill'.

1 Write definitions for the following pairs of words. You may use a dictionary.

a remark _____

_____

re-mark _____

b redress _____

re-dress _____

c recreate _____

_____

re-create _____

2 Underline the errors in the following sentences and write the correct word in the space provided.

a Dad bought some antifreeze to deice the car windscreen.

_____

b Kevin's mum had to re-sign as president of the basketball club because she punched a referee.

_____

c There is no way that the local council will reelect a criminal.

_____

Writing and creating tools

Writing task

Write a physical description of a family member or a character from a novel, TV show or film. Your description should be 120 words and include the following:

- description of their clothing, shoes, hair, jewellery, make-up and any distinguishing physical features

- at least 10 different adjectives.

1 **Research** – If writing about a family member, spend some time with them. Think about the things that make them different from other people.

2 **Plan** – Number the information in the order you want it in your description.

3 **Draft** – Write your draft, including ten different adjectives.

4 **Edit and proofread** – Check that you have used at least 10 different adjectives in your description. Check spelling and punctuation. Read over your description. Does it provide a complete description of the person or character you are writing about?

Creating task

Explore **multimodal presentation methods** for your description.

- If you have access to the free downloadable program Microsoft Photo Story 3, turn your description into a **digital story** combining words with photos of the person you have described.

Listen and respond to what other students have done.

- Read your description to the class.

- **Reflect on** the language choices made by your classmates. In small groups make lists of the different adjectives used in your description and the nouns that they describe. Select the top 10 effective adjectives and add these to your word bank for future writing.

Unit  4

Persuasive texts: Speeches

Tools in this unit

- Reading tools: Understanding the speech by Nina Marshallsea
- Grammar tools: Adjectives of degree
- Vocabulary tools: Persuasive language techniques
- Spelling tools: Five rules for forming comparative and superlative adjectives
- Punctuation tools: Commas
- Writing and creating tools: Write a one-minute speech

Modes covered

- Receptive: Reading, listening and viewing
- Productive: Speaking, writing and creating

Cross-curriculum priorities

- Sustainability

General capabilities

- Literacy
- Information and communication technology capability
- Critical and creative thinking
- Ethical understanding

Curriculum content in this unit

- Language for interaction: ACELA1541, ACELA1542
- Text structure and organisation: ACELA1766, ACELA1766, ACELA1544
- Expressing and developing ideas: ACELA1545, ACELA1547
- Responding to literature: ACELT1807
- Examining literature: ACELT1630, ACELT1767
- Interacting with others: ACELY1730, ACELY1808, ACELY1731
- Interpreting, analysing, evaluating: ACELY1732, ACELY1733, ACELY1734, ACELY1735
- Creating texts: ACELY1736, ACELY1810, ACELY1738

Responding to texts

Speech by Nina Marshallsea to Local Council

Good evening Councillors and fellow community members

My name is Nina Marshallsea. On May 14 this year my thirteen-year-old daughter, Constance, was walking our dog Molly along the footpath when an official from this council handed her a ticket for a $3900 fine.

We moved here to Tassie, from Victoria early this year. We are responsible dog owners. Molly has been desexed, microchipped and she was on a lead when Constance was fined. Our dog Molly is a Japanese Tosa or Inu that we rescued five years ago from Saveadognow in Melbourne. While Molly is bigger and heavier than some dogs, she is more likely to lick you to death than bite you. She is the most beautiful, best and most obedient dog.

Yet we were fined $3900 because here in Tasmania Molly is considered a Restricted Breed Dog and required to have an approved collar and can only be walked by a person over 18 years old with a lead less than two metres in length.

Every Victorian knows about the tragic death of Ayen Choi in 2011. She was mauled by a pitbull-mastiff cross. However, the Japanese Tosa is a mastiff, not a pitbull-bull mastiff cross. Molly weighs only 36kg and stands only 62cm. She is considered one of the smallest of her breed.

The DogInfo and Rescue dog websites do not list the Japanese Tosa as a Restricted Dog Breed. Molly is not on the Restricted Dog Breed list in New South Wales or Victoria.

We had no idea that Molly is on the Restricted Dog Breed list in Tasmania. I think that it's unfair that all the states in Australia don't have the same Restricted Dog Breed lists. It's like saying that a person who kills someone else is considered a murderer in New South Wales but not even a criminal in Western Australia. Every state in Australia should have the same Restricted Dog Breed list.

I know that we are all reasonable citizens here and I request that this council withdraw the fine and give us a warning instead.

Councillors and community members, I thank you for listening.

Understanding the speech by Nina Marshallsea

Read the **speech by Nina Marshallsea to Local Council** then answer the following questions. You may use a dictionary.

1 Where does the speech take place?

....

2 What does Nina Marshallsea want to happen?

....

3 List three of the adjectives Nina Marshallsea uses to describe their dog.

....

4 What is Nina Marshallsea's argument about the Restricted Dog Breed list?

....

....

5 Tick one box only to answer each of the following questions:

a Which word best describes the text by Nina Marshallsea?

a letter ❑

a report ❑

a speech ❑

b Which do you think most accurately describes the purpose of this text?

to persuade the councillors to withdraw the fine ❑

to instruct the councillors to issue warnings not fines ❑

to inform the councillors about Restricted Dog Breed lists ❑

Grammar tools

Adjectives of degree

Adjectives can tell to what degree (or extent) a noun or pronoun is being described.

Adjectives of degree are an important part of persuasive writing and will help you to express your opinions more accurately.

There are three forms of adjectives of degree:

1 **Positive form** (found in a dictionary) describes only one noun (person or thing).

Example: My park has a big swing.   noun = park   adjective = big

2 **Comparative form** compares two nouns.

Example: My park has the bigger swing.

3 **Superlative form** compares more than two nouns.

Example: My park has the biggest swing.

More examples:

Positive	Comparative	Superlative
small	smaller	smallest
beautiful	more beautiful	most beautiful
many	more	most
bad	worse	worst
good	better	best
interesting	more interesting	most interesting

1 List the four **superlative adjectives** in the speech.

....

2 List the two **comparative adjectives** in the speech.

....

3 Complete the table by writing the comparative and superlative forms of these adjectives.

Positive	Comparative	Superlative
brave		
kind		
generous		
hopeful		
mad		

Persuasive language techniques

Persuasive language presents an argument to the reader or audience.

The overall goal of persuasive writing is to persuade you **to agree** with its point of view on a topic or issue. Persuasive language is used in speeches, letters to the editor, opinion articles and cartoons.

The list below introduces you to some persuasive language techniques or devices.

Facts	Statements that can be proven to be true
Opinions	A person's thoughts or point of view about a topic. These may or may not include facts
Statistics and evidence	Figures and percentages that can be used as evidence. Always check that they are accurate
Generalisations	Sweeping statements that start with 'all' or 'every'
Exaggeration	An overstatement of a point that cannot be measured or proven
Inclusive language	Language that tries to include the reader, e.g. 'we', 'our', 'us'

1 Nina Marshallsea uses exaggeration to persuade the councillors. Quote the example of this technique in her speech.

----

2 List the two facts Nina Marshallsea uses to support her point about Restricted Dog Breed lists.

---

3 Quote the generalisation used by Nina Marshallsea.

---

4 Quote one of the opinions Nina Marshallsea gives.

Spelling tools

Five rules for forming comparative and superlative adjectives

The following rules will help you to form comparative and superlative adjectives correctly:

1 If the adjective ends in **'e'** add **'r'** or **'st'**.

Example: safe ➡ safer ➡ safest

2 If the adjective ends in **'y'** change **'y'** to **'i'** and add **'er'** or **'est'**.

Example: lazy ➡ lazier ➡ laziest

3 If the adjective ends in a consonant with a single vowel before it, double the consonant.

Example: sad ➡ sadder ➡ saddest

4 For other endings add **'er'** or **'est'**.

Example: fast ➡ faster ➡ fastest

5 In general, for adjectives of two or more syllables, **'more'** and **'most'** are used.

Example: careful ➡ more careful ➡ most careful

1 Write the comparative forms of the following adjectives in the spaces provided.

a handsome _____

b late _____

c pleasant _____

d many _____

e cautious _____

f bad _____

2 Write the superlative forms of the following adjectives in the spaces provided.

a good _____

b happy _____

c difficult _____

d small _____

e gorgeous _____

f generous _____

3 Write the positive forms of the following adjectives in the spaces provided.

a wildest _____

b most comfortable _____

c best _____

d easier _____

e worse _____

f more complex _____

Punctuation tools

Commas

Commas make sentences easier to read and understand. Commas are used for four main reasons when you are writing.

Four rules for commas

1 Commas are used to show readers where to pause and take breath when reading a sentence.

Example: The woman explained to her child that the Mayor had made the wrong decision about the park, but there was no turning back.

2 Commas are used to separate the name of a person from the rest of the sentence.

Example: Julie, please move away from the sandpit.

3 Commas are needed to separate words in a list.

Example: Julie likes playing on the swings, slide, monkey bars and ropes.

4 Commas are used to mark the beginning of direct speech (words actually spoken).

Example: The Mayor said, 'Begin digging Mr Foreman.'

1 These sentences need commas to make them easier to read and understand. Add them where you think they belong. Some sentences may require more than one comma. Hint: reading the sentence aloud will help you locate the right place for the comma.

a Punctuation is full of apostrophes commas full stops and quotation marks.

b The poster said 'New carpark set to open in record time!'

c 'Where did you park the car Luke?'

d My mum replied 'I miss the park too!'

e I remember a really special day I spent at the park running laughing singing and playing with my friends.

Writing task

Write a one-minute speech (approximately 200 words) to deliver to your class on one of the following topics:

- Owners of Restricted Dog Breeds should be charged if their dog injures anyone.

- The lists for Restricted Dog Breeds should be the same all over Australia.

Be sure to include persuasive language techniques in your speech, including superlative adjectives, generalisations, opinions, statistics (made up) and exaggeration.

1 **Research** – Find out about Restricted Dog Breeds and map out your own speech. Consider the following:

- What will be your main argument or message?

- Who is your audience? Who are you trying to persuade that this is a good idea?

- Why are you giving this speech? (to persuade)

- The tone and style of your piece (serious, formal or confident).

  ----

2 **Plan** – Number your points in the order you want them to appear in your speech for maximum persuasive impact.

3 **Draft** – Write your speech.

4 **Edit and proofread** – Check that your speech follows a logical order. Check spelling and punctuation and that you can deliver your speech in the allocated time limit. Do you think you will have persuaded your readers to see things from your point of view?

Creating task

Explore **multimodal presentation methods** for your speech.

* Take the major points from your speech and turn it into a PowerPoint presentation that combines photos of dogs alongside the main points of your argument.

* If you have access to a **digital video camera** or **video function** on your digital camera, make a short video about your point of view about the topic of Restricted Dog Breeds.

Listen and respond to what other students have done.

* Deliver your speech to the class.

* Ask your class to identify the persuasive techniques used in the speeches. Comment on which techniques were the most persuasive and give reasons why.

Revision tools: Units 1–4

Complete these questions by yourself. You may use a dictionary.

Grammar tools

Christmas holiday

I went to my uncle's small farm for Christmas in Wattlesea. I saw a giant flock of birds and a gaggle of noisy geese. I milked a herd of stinky cows and I suffered from exhaustion! I think that happiness is living near a sandy beach.

1 Read the 'Christmas holiday' text above and list the following:

a five common nouns _____

_____

b two proper nouns _____

c two abstract nouns _____

d three collective nouns _____

2 List the six main verbs in 'Christmas holiday'.

_____

_____

3 Complete the following directions to the dairy by adding the correct prepositions.

Walk _____ the hill _____ the farmhouse.

Proceed _____ the path for 50 metres.

Walk _____ a small bridge and turn left.

You will see the dairy standing _____ a hill and _____ a road.

Vocabulary tools

4 Divide the following words into syllables using a forward slash.

Example: vam / pire

a cemetery _____

b disaster _____

c circus _____

d alien _____

5 What type of informal language are the words 'bogan' and 'chick'?

_____

Spelling tools

6 Rewrite the misspelt words correctly in the spaces provided.

a emenies _____

b trecherous _____

c nuckle _____

d rubarb _____

e rinoceros _____

f desparate _____

g fatel _____

h rist _____

i ritgt _____

j potatos _____

Unit  5

Literary texts: Characters

Tools in this unit

- Reading tools: Understanding *The Declaration*
- Grammar tools: Verbs
- Vocabulary tools: Features of literary texts
- Spelling tools: Doubling the final consonant – words that end in 'l' or 't'
- Punctuation tools: Paragraphs and topic sentences
- Writing and creating tools: Construct a character profile

Modes covered

- Receptive: Reading and listening
- Productive: Speaking, writing and creating

General capabilities

- Literacy
- Personal and social capability
- Information and communication technology capability
- Critical and creative thinking
- Ethical understanding

Curriculum content in this unit

- Language for interaction: ACELA1541
- Text structure and organisation: ACELA1766, ACELA1809, ACELA1544
- Expressing and developing ideas: ACELA1547
- Literature and context: ACELT1626
- Responding to literature: ACELT1627, ACELT1807
- Examining literature: ACELT1629, ACELT1767
- Creating literature: ACELT1768
- Interacting with others: ACELY1808, ACELY1731
- Interpreting, analysing, evaluating: ACELY1732, ACELY1733, ACELY1735
- Creating texts: ACELY1736, ACELY1810, ACELY1738

Responding to texts

The Declaration by Gemma Malley (2007)

11 January, 2140

My name is Anna.

My name is Anna and I shouldn't be here. I shouldn't exist.

But I do.

It's not my fault I'm here. I didn't ask to be born. But that doesn't make it any better that I was. They caught me early, though which bodes well. That's what Mrs Pincent says, anyway. She's the lady that runs Grange Hall. We call her House Matron. Grange Hall is where I live. Where people like me are brought up to be Useful – the 'best of a bad situation', Mrs Pincent says.

I don't have another name. Not like Mrs Pincent does. Mrs Pincent's name is Margaret Pincent. Some people call her Margaret, most people call her Mrs Pincent, and we call her House Matron. Lately I've started to call her Mrs Pincent too, although not to her face – I'm not stupid.

Legal people generally have at least two names, sometimes more.

Not me, though. I'm just Anna. People like me don't need more than one name, Mrs Pincent says. One is quite enough.

Source: Malley, G. 2007, *The Declaration*, Bloomsbury, London, pp. 1-2.

Understanding *The Declaration*

Read the extract from **The Declaration** and answer the following questions. You may use a dictionary.

1   How do you know that this extract is a diary entry?

....

2   When does this story take place?

....

3   What are two things you learn about Anna in this extract?

....

....

4   How do you know that Anna's situation is not a good one to be in?

....

....

5   What do you think Grange Hall is? Why?

....

....

6   What is Mrs Pincent's role?

....

Grammar tools

Verbs

Verbs are doing, being or having words.

Examples: I jump, you have, I think, we own, I am

Verbs show the action that takes place.

There are three types of verbs:

1 Verbs made up of one word are called **main verbs**.

Example: breathe

2 Verbs made up of two or more words are called **compound verbs**. A compound verb is made by adding an auxiliary verb (or two).

Example: is breathing

3 An **auxiliary verb** is a helper verb but may also stand alone like a main verb.

Example: Anna **was** scared.

Other examples of auxiliary verbs:

am   did   may   were   are   do   will   must   been   shall   could   have   was

Note this:
All sentences must contain a verb.

- A sentence is a group of words that makes sense on its own. All sentences contain a **subject** and a **predicate**.

- The subject is the person or thing that takes the action that the verb describes.

Example: **Anna** is trained at Grange Hall.

- The predicate tells us what the subject is or does. It includes the verb of the sentence.

Example: Anna **is trained at Grange Hall**. (Verb: *is trained*.)

1 Complete the following sentences by adding main verbs from the box below.

| blows | walks | told | crawls |

a Ben's mother _____ him to stay away from the locked door.

b Ben _____ around the room in circles.

c The spider _____ onto his hand.

d The wind _____ icy cold through the open window.

2 Complete these sentences by adding **auxiliary verbs**.

a Ben _____ sleeping when the cat broke the vase.

b Mother _____ lost patience with the cat.

c I _____ wake up early tomorrow so I can eat breakfast with Dad.

3 Rewrite the **subject** in the following sentences in the space provided.

a Ben hid in the cupboard. _____

b Two spiders crawled slowly up the windowsill. _____

c Mother called us to come inside before it started to rain. _____

d The wind was the coldest all winter. _____

4 Rewrite the **predicate** of the following sentences in the space provided.

a I walked outside and picked some flowers from the garden.

_____

b While trapped in the cupboard, Ben recited the alphabet 10 times.

_____

c Too scared to speak, I sat shaking in the corner of the room.

_____

Vocabulary tools

Features of literary texts

Literary texts include novels, poems, film scripts, short stories and memoirs. Literary texts have certain features or key elements that you will become more familiar with as you read them.

Key terms are listed below.

Author and title

The person who has written a text and the name of a text.

Characters

The people, animals or creatures in a text. Characters may be alive or dead, seen or unseen, silent or vocal.

Narrative

A story that is either **fictional** or **non-fictional**. It tells us what happened through descriptions that draw the reader or viewer into the world of the text.

Protagonist

The main character in a text who may encounter problems but is usually the narrative's hero or heroine.

Point of view

The opinion or perspective being offered by the author or a character in the narrative.

Style

The way a text is written. This includes elements such as language, tone, genre, point of view and structure.

Theme(s)

The message(s) in a text. What the author is trying to tell the reader.

Setting

Where and when a narrative takes place.

Context

The background to a story, including the author's experiences and why they want to write the narrative.

Genre

A particular type or form of text. *Examples:* horror, science fiction, romance

Plot

The events of a narrative, in order.

Tone

The author's attitude towards the subject. *Example:* the author may write with a critical tone or a sympathetic tone.

1   Referring only to the extract from ***The Declaration***, answer the following questions.

a   Who is the author of ***The Declaration***?

....

b   Who are the characters that appear in this extract?

....

c   Who is the protagonist in this extract? What problem has she encountered?

....

d   What is the setting of this extract?

....

e   Use three adjectives to describe the style of this extract including its genre, language and tone.

....

....

Spelling tools

Doubling the final consonant – words that end in 'l' or 't'

Words with double 'l' or double 't' require particular attention when you are spelling them.

There are **five rules** you should follow:

1 A word may change from having a single 'l' to having a double 'l' when a suffix is added.

Example: travel + ed = **travelled**

2 If there are two vowels (a, e, i, o, u) before the final 'l' you do not double the 'l' before adding a suffix.

Example: fool + ed = **fooled**

3 With some words that end in 'al', do not double the 'l' when adding a suffix.

Example: capital + ism = **capitalism**

4 If the vowel sound before the 't' is short, double the 't' when adding a suffix.

Example: rot + en = **rotten**

5 If the vowel sound before the 't' is long, do not double the 't' when adding a suffix.

Example: greet + ing = **greeting**

If in doubt, consult a dictionary or *The Cambridge Guide to English Usage*.

1 Rewrite the following words adding the suffix in brackets.

a school (ing) _____

b quit (ing) _____

c enrol (ed) _____

d suit (ed) _____

e unveil (ed) ....

f travel (er) ....

g imperial (ism) ....

h trial (ed) ....

2 Underline the spelling mistakes in the following sentences and write the correctly spelt words in the spaces provided.

a Susan found herself rebeling against her mother when she told her to clean her room.

....

b Will everybody please be seatted.

....

c Coraline was labeled strange by the boys in her class because she talked to spiders.

....

d When they unveilled what was hidden behind the secret door, everyone swivelled their heads to look.

....

Punctuation tools

Paragraphs and topic sentences

Paragraphs are an essential part of effective writing.

1 A paragraph consists of a sentence or sentences grouped together because they are about the same thought or idea. These sentences must relate to one another.

2 Each paragraph has a **topic sentence** that expresses the main point.

3 Paragraphs help you to order your ideas so that a reader can best understand what you mean.

4 A new paragraph is indicated by leaving a line between each paragraph or by indenting at the start of the paragraph.

You should begin a new paragraph when:

- you start writing about a new topic or make a new point in your essay

- you are writing dialogue and a new or different person speaks.

A **topic sentence** introduces the main point or focus of the paragraph. It is usually the opening sentence of the paragraph.

1 The following extract from **'The Declaration'** has had the paragraphs removed. Indicate where you think the paragraphs should be by marking your suggested breaks with an asterisk (*).

That's when the dying stopped, first in Europe, America and China and then, gradually, everywhere else. Some countries were late adopters because the drugs were expensive, but then terrorists started to attack England because they wouldn't give everyone the drug and soon after that the price got lower so everyone could have them. 'And what do you think happened, then?' Mr Sargent always asked, his beady eyes searching out someone in the classroom who would encapsulate the fundamental flaw in the programme. More times than not, Anna would put up her hand. 'There were too many people,' she would say seriously. 'If no one dies and people have more children, there's nowhere for everyone to go.'

Malley, G. 2007, *The Declaration*, Bloomsbury, London, pp. 1–2.

2 Below are four topics. Choose one and write a short paragraph (4–6 sentences) about it. Begin with a strong topic sentence to open your paragraph.

grandma   my best friend   a family pet   my favourite TV character

----

Writing and creating tools

Writing task

What is your favourite story? Construct a detailed character profile for a character in this story. Your character profile should be 200 words.

1 **Research** – Choose your character. Use the following characteristics to begin constructing your profile. Take brief notes for each:

- Name of character

  ....

- Physical appearance

  ....

- What they say and think

  ....

- What they do

  ....

- What others say about them

  ....

- Goals

  ....

- Problems they face

  ....

- Do they have an enemy?

  ....

- How they change from the start of the story to the finish of the story

  ....

2 **Plan** – Decide the order in which the information will appear in your profile. Check that you have covered all the different aspects of your chosen character. Include quotations from the text.

3 **Draft** – Begin writing your character profile, turning your notes into sentences and then clear paragraphs.

4 **Edit and proofread** – Check that you have used paragraphs correctly, as well as quotations to support the statements in your profile. Check your spelling and punctuation. Does each paragraph have a topic sentence? Have you used verbs to show your character in action?

Creating task

Explore **multimodal presentation methods** for your character profile.

- Imagine that you are the character you have written about and start a **character blog**. Write using **first person** pronouns such as 'I' and 'my'. Use your imagination to create new information about this character. You may even wish to imagine an alternative ending to his/her story.

- Turn your character profile into a PowerPoint presentation that includes extracts from the text to help illustrate the points you are making about the character. Record yourself reading these extracts and include them in your presentation as a sound file.

Listen and respond to what other students have done.

- Deliver your finished character profile as an **oral presentation** to the class. In addition to reading it aloud, briefly describe how you planned your profile.

- Compare the characters' features and motivations and how these change. Explain which character interests you the most and why.

Unit

Informal writing: Emails

Tools in this unit

- Reading tools: Understanding 'Boxing Day Test' email
- Grammar tools: Verb tense
- Vocabulary tools: Informal language
- Spelling tools: Changing verb tense
- Punctuation tools: Writing numbers
- Writing and creating tools: Write an informal email to a friend

Modes covered

- Receptive: Reading and listening
- Productive: Speaking, writing and creating

General capabilities

- Literacy
- Information and communication technology capability
- Critical and creative thinking
- Numeracy

Curriculum content in this unit

- Language for interaction: ACELA1541
- Text structure and organisation: ACELA1766, ACELA1809, ACELA1544
- Expressing and developing ideas: ACELA1547, ACELA1549
- Texts in context: ACELY1729
- Interacting with others: ACELY1808, ACELY1731
- Interpreting, analysing, evaluating: ACELY1733, ACELY1734, ACELY1735
- Creating texts: ACELY1736, ACELY1810, ACELY1738

Responding to texts

Boxing Day Test, email

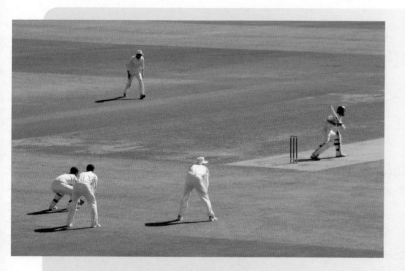

To: Jack O'Hara

From: Tom Jocovich

Subject: Boxing Day Test

Hey Jack,

How are things in London, mate? As you know, I'm a cricket tragic! So is my fave aunt. She shouted me an airfare from Sydney and a ticket to the famous Boxing Day Test, Pakistan vs Australia, in Melbourne. I was rapt! (Did I tell you, I'm a fast (sometimes) bowler and play in the Under 15s.)

So anyway, back to the match. Aussie captain Michael Clarke won the toss and we batted first. The openers were Katich and Watson. The Pakistani team missed a slips catch. They had a 17-year-old left-arm pace bowler, Aamer. He wore a white headband like the great D.K. Lillee from the 70s. I thought headbands were dorky but it looked cool on him. Aamer conceded only 10 runs from his first six-over spell!

Their spinner bowled offies and a couple of doozras but our batsmen were too good. While I bought hot chips and two meat pies, Watson went out for 93 runs. I was really hoping he would make a ton. Clarke scored 50 off 55 balls. His half-century came when he drove to mid-on in the 81st over.

The atmosphere was great. I watched the bogans in Bay 13. Do you have bogans in London? They threw an inflatable beach ball around until the security guards finally caught it. A group of them were painted blue and dressed like Smurfs!

At the end of the day Aussies were 3–305.

Maybe if I wear a white headband I will bowl faster?

Anyway, gotta go. Email me back soon as you can, mate. Have you been to the soccer, I mean football, recently?

Thommo ☺

Understanding 'Boxing Day Test' email

Read **'Boxing Day Test'** and answer the following questions. You may use a dictionary.

1 Who are the two teams playing cricket?

....

2 Who is Michael Clarke?

....

3 List four facts given about Aamer.

....

....

....

4 What did Thommo eat at the cricket?

....

5 Tick one box only for each of the following questions:

a What type of text is **'Boxing Day Test'**?

short story ❑   poem ❑   email ❑

b Who is the intended audience for **'Boxing Day Test'**?

a friend ❑   cricket fans ❑   bogans ❑

c Which best describes the purpose for writing this text?

to persuade Jack to go to the cricket   ❑

to describe Thommo's day at the cricket   ❑

to inform Jack about how cricket is played ❑

Grammar tools

Verb tense

Verbs are doing, being or having words. They tell us the action that has occurred. The verb's **tense** tells **when** the action has taken place.

There are three major tenses to be aware of:

1 **Past tense** tells you what has happened in the past.

Example: Tom **wrote** an email to Jack.

2 **Present tense** tells you what is happening now.

Example: Tom **writes** an email to Jack or Tom **is writing** an email to Jack.

3 **Future tense** tells you what will happen in the future.

Example: Tom **will write** an email to Jack after the cricket match.

The tense is indicated by **verb endings** and **auxiliary verbs** (helping verbs).

	Past (What happened?)	Present (What's happening now?)	Future (What will happen?)
Examples	wrote	writes/is writing	will write
Verb endings	en n t ed	ing s	
Auxiliary verbs	was had were has	is are am	will shall might may should could

1 List the nine different verbs in paragraph 2 of **'Boxing Day Test'** in the space below.

_____

_____

_____

_____

_____

2 Write the verbs from question 1 in the following table, then add their present and future tense forms. The first one has been done for you.

Present tense	Past tense	Future tense
win, is winning	won	will win

Vocabulary tools

Informal language

Informal language, when used in written texts, is a casual style of writing closer to the conventions of conversation. It is often used in blogs, journals, emails and letters to friends and family.

Informal language can include:

visual writing techniques   interjections   SMS conventions   abbreviations

slang   colloquialisms   jargon

Slang is language specific to a particular country or region. Australia has its own 'slang vocabulary', as do other countries.

Example: 'bogan'

Colloquialisms are words and phrases that are informal, popular and in current usage. Unlike slang, colloquialisms are often more universal.

Example: 'cool'

Jargon is language used for specific audiences like sports groups, computer-users, people who do specialised work and members of subcultures. Jargon differs from slang and colloquialisms because it is often associated with a group or subculture that transcends national or regional borders.

Example: 'hang time' in basketball

Something you should know about jargon:

• it can include everyday words that have been given other, different meanings.

Example: while 'bug' is a word for an insect, as a part of computer jargon it also refers to an error in computer software.

1 Write each example of cricket jargon from the box beside its correct meaning.

toss   openers   offie   doozra   ton   half-century   mid-on

a 100 runs ....

b position on the field ....

c type of ball bowled at the batsman ....

d another type of ball bowled at the batsman ....

e two players who bat first ....

f 50 runs ....

g throwing a coin and calling heads or tails ....

2 Write formal English words for the following slang and colloquial terms.

a chick ....

b suss ....

c wimp ....

d shout ....

e some random ....

f dodgy ....

g amazeballs ....

h probs ....

3 Identify a sport, interest or hobby that you are interested in. Brainstorm for five minutes and list as many jargon terms related to that sport, interest or hobby that you can think of.

....

....

....

....

....

Spelling tools

Changing verb tense

To change a verb's form from present to past tense you should follow these rules:

1 Add 'ed' to present tense verbs.

Example: laugh – laughed

2 If a present tense verb ends in 'y', change 'y' to 'i' and add 'ed'.

Example: cry – cried

3 If a present tense verb ends in 'e', add 'd'.

Example: provide – provided

4 If a present tense verb ends with a single consonant, double the consonant and add 'ed'.

Example: bat – batted

There are some exceptions to these rules. Here are a few of them:

know – knew   eat – ate   teach – taught   meet – met

1 Complete the following verb tense table.

Present tense verbs	Past tense verbs
lose	
	made
jump	
drive	
	walked
bleed	
	swam
try	
	closed

2 This journal entry should be written with present tense verbs. Underline the 10 incorrectly used verbs and rewrite them in the space provided.

30/12/09 I hated cricket! It's sooo boring and always will take forever! Men weared dorky costumes, spitted lots and sometimes hitted a ball a bowler thrown at them. When cricket was on TV my brother, Thommo, wented nuts! So did my aunt but she's older so a little nuts is OK. I wished cricketers played football!

Punctuation tools

Writing numbers

In general, you should write all numbers below 10 in words.

Examples: one, three, seven, nine

Numbers over 100 can appear as numerical digits.

Examples: 100, 150, 202, 350

Here are some more conventions for writing numerical digits:

- sums of money: $25.50
- percentages: 100%
- times: 5.30 am, 11 o'clock
- word counts: 200 words
- mathematical sums: 5 × 10 = 50
- sports scores: 14 points per game

- weights and measures: 5 kg, 5 km
- dates: 16 August 1996
- temperatures: 42 degrees or 42°
- addresses: 16 Magnolia Court
- crowd numbers: 25,000 fans

1   Answer the following questions about **'Boxing Day Test'** by writing numbers.

a   What age group cricket team does Thommo play in? ....

b   How old is the fast bowler from Pakistan? ....

c   How many runs did Watson go out for? ....

d   During what 'over' did Clarke make his 50 runs? ....

2 Rewrite the following writing numerical digits and numbers in words where appropriate.

Saturday August twenty fourth

OMG! I'm totally confused about when to write numbers and when to write words.

Do I live at six Gipps Ave? It's a number under 10. What if I only write 9 words for an essay? (Yep. I know I'll fail if I write less than five hundred words) Do I weigh 54 kg? Did I join fourteen thousand other screaming teenagers and pay a hundred dollars to see Pink in concert? Did I get eighty percent for Maths? (as if!) It's soo confusing. Did I score twenty points in the basketball game? Two hundred dollars looks a lot more than $200 when it's written in words. Is it ten o'clock? Whatever. It's past my bedtime. Bye sis. 2x

---

Writing and creating tools

Writing task

Write an informal email to a friend about a sporting event or other special interest event that you have attended. Your email should be 200 words. (You don't actually have to send this email.)

In your email, include the following:

- informal language

- your feelings about the event and the people involved.

1 **Research** – Choose your topic. Write answers to the following:

- Where did the event take place?

  ....

- What happened?

  ....

- What was the atmosphere like?

  ....

- How did you feel? What did you see and hear?

  ....

2 **Plan** – As you take notes in your own workbook on the above points, consider: what the message of your email will be; what the purpose of your email is; who your audience is; and the style and tone you intend to write it in.

3 **Draft** – Write a draft of your informal email.

4 **Edit and proofread** – Read over your email. Is your information written in a logical order? Check that you have used informal language, that you have written numbers correctly, if these are used, and that you have used paragraphs correctly. Are your verbs written in the correct tense?

Creating task

Explore **multimodal presentation methods** for informal writing.

- If you are part of a sports team or do some other regular activity, create an **online journal** or **blog** that makes use of informal language to record your experiences on a weekly basis.

- Broadcast your experiences with a three-minute **podcast**, e.g. 'At the chess club'.

- If you can access the free downloadable program Microsoft Photo Story 3, use it to create your own **digital story** with text and images based on the events in your email or other personal informal writing pieces.

Listen and respond to what other students have done.

- Deliver your finished email as an **oral presentation** to the class.

- Write a 50-word summary of one of the presentations you have listened to, giving particular attention to the informal language that has been used.

- Identify five different examples of informal language used by your classmates. Add these examples to your own informal language and visual writing vocabulary lists.

Unit

Responsive writing: Film reviews

Tools in this unit

- Reading tools: Understanding the film review of *The Hunger Games*
- Grammar tools: Adverbs
- Vocabulary tools: Film vocabulary
- Spelling tools: Turning adjectives into adverbs
- Punctuation tools: Style guide for writing a film review
- Writing and creating tools: Write a film review

Modes covered

- Receptive: Reading, listening and writing
- Productive: Speaking, writing and creating

General capabilities

- Literacy
- Personal and social capability
- Information and communication technology capability
- Critical and creative thinking

Curriculum content in this unit

- Language for interaction: ACELA1541, ACELA1542
- Text structure and organisation: ACELA1766, ACELA1809
- Expressing and developing ideas: ACELA1547, ACELA1549
- Responding to literature: ACELT1628
- Examining literature: ACELT1629, ACELT1630
- Creating literature: ACELT1632, ACELT1768
- Texts in context: ACELY1729
- Interacting with others: ACELY1808, ACELY1731
- Interpreting, analysing, evaluating: ACELY1732, ACELY1733
- Creating texts: ACELY1736, ACELY1810, ACELY1738

Responding to texts

The Hunger Games (directed by Gary Ross, 2012)

The Hunger Games is a film based on the first book of a trilogy written by Suzanne Collins of the same title. It is the 13th highest-grossing film generating almost $700 million, and has won over ten awards. Those who have read the book would know that the story is a fascinating mix between science-fiction and action. Instead of being about alien life forms or foreign galaxies, the story provides a hypothesis of the future in the continent of North America.

This future civilisation, called Panem, is divided up into thirteen sections – twelve Districts and the Capitol. Each year, two teenaged Tributes from each District are selected randomly to compete in the Hunger Games, a gladiator-like fight to the death which is televised throughout Panem. On the day of Reaping, when the selection takes place, the protagonist, Katniss Everdeen (Jennifer Lawrence) courageously volunteers to compete instead of her sister, Primrose (Willow Shields), who was chosen.

Katniss, and the male Tribute, Peeta Mellark (Josh Hutcherson) are then quickly whisked away to the Capitol, where they undergo training, and taste the typical indulgent Capitol way of life, which is so different to their basic and unprivileged existence in the Districts. Not long after, they find themselves within the Hunger Games Arena, a space where natural elements are digitally manipulated by the Game makers in the Capitol. It is here that they must all fight both the Arena and each other to survive and become the victor.

The Hunger Games showcases courage, powerful love, bitter hatred and needless distrust, fear and social inequality in a very creative and vivid fashion. Both Katniss and Peeta display amazing drive and persistence, and, in the end, it is their love for each other that keeps them alive.

I enjoyed the book immensely, and, unlike many other adapted books, I enjoyed the film as well. At two-and-a-quarter hours in length (which in my opinion is too long), it explains some elements not explained in the book. We find out how (spoiler alert): Peeta loses his leg, Katniss goes deaf in one ear, she gets the Mockingjay pin from one of her friends, and about the Tesserae, the place where teenagers living in the Districts can enter their name more than once to receive oil and grain for a year.

I was also disappointed with the fire special effects. On the other hand, for those who have not read the books, it provides a satisfactory introduction to the trilogy.

I give this film a score of three stars.

Reviewed by P. Snow (pen name)

Reading tools

Understanding the film review of *The Hunger Games*

Read the **film review**, then answer the following questions. You may use a dictionary.

1 Who is the director of the film being reviewed?

....

2 Explain the following terms: 'Hunger Games', Tributes, Panem, Reaping

....

....

....

....

3 Who is the film's protagonist? What is the name of the actor who plays her?

....

....

4 Describe the genre of the film.

----

5 What are the themes or messages of the film?

----

6 What are two differences between the book and the film versions?

----

7 What criticisms does the reviewer have of the film?

✂ Grammar tools

Adverbs

Adverbs add meaning to verbs to explain how, when and where the action takes place.

There are three main types of adverbs.

1 Manner – how an action is performed.

Example: He walked **slowly**.

2 Time – when an action is performed.

Example: He walked **yesterday**.

3 Place – where an action is performed.

Example: He walked **outside**.

The table below lists some more examples of adverbs. Most adverbs of manner can be formed by adding 'ly' to an adjective (see Spelling tools, p. 87).

Manner (how)	Time (when)	Place (where)
bravely	never	everywhere
fast	recently	anywhere
lazily	always	nowhere
noisily	presently	there

Fix it!

'Well' is an adverb. *Example:* The clever student performed well in their exam.

'Good' is an adjective. *Example:* A good student does their homework regularly.

It is incorrect to say, 'The clever student performed good in their exam.'

1 List the five adverbs of manner in the **film review** in the space below.

....

....

2 Complete the table with the five adverbs above and the verbs they are describing in the **film review**.

Paragraph number	Adverb	Verb
2	randomly	chosen
2		
3		
3		
5		

3 Write each of the five adverbs from question 1 in a sentence of your own, using different verbs to the ones used in the review.

Film vocabulary

When you speak and write about film texts you should practise using the correct film vocabulary. An introductory list of film vocabulary is provided below.

Director	The person who makes decisions about each scene and the overall film
Cinematographer	The person in charge of camera work
Lighting	Colours, shadows
Camera shots	Any of a variety of shots used to tell the story, including close-up, extreme close-up, wide shot and tracking shot
Genre	A specific type of film, e.g. Western, comedy, etc.
Editing	Putting together shots in a sequential form to tell the story
Location	The place where a scene is shot
Dialogue	Words and lines spoken by characters in a film
Motif	An image or object repeated throughout a film for effect
Sound effects	Sounds other than music and dialogue
Mise-en-scene	All the elements literally put within a scene, including characters, props and sets

1 Add to your key film vocabulary by researching definitions of the following terms.

a special effects

....

....

....

b voice-over

....

....

c screenplay

....

....

d point-of-view shot

....

....

Spelling tools

Turning adjectives into adverbs

An adjective can easily be changed into an adverb where it is appropriate to do so.

The rules below will help you to do this correctly.

Four rules

1 Add 'ly' to the adjective.

Example: quick + ly = quickly

2 If the adjective ends in 'le', drop 'le' and add 'ly'.

Example: sensible – 'le' + 'ly' = sensibly

3 If the adjective ends in 'y', change 'y' to 'i' and then add 'ly'.

Example: lazy – change 'y' to 'i' and add 'ly' = lazily

4 If the adjective ends in 'ic', add 'ally'.

Example: romantic + ally = romantically

Exceptions to these rules: well, hard, fast

Note this:

Only one word ends in 'icly': publicly.

1 Change the following adjectives into adverbs (manner).

a serious _____

b swift _____

c noble _____

d desperate _____

e feeble _____

f hasty _____

2 Write two sentences using four of the adverbs (manner) you made in question 1. Include adverbs of time and place to make your sentences more interesting, if you like.

_____

_____

_____

_____

_____

3 Change the following adjectives into adverbs following the correct rule.

a magic _____

b problematic _____

c slow _____

d emphatic _____

e fanatic _____

f cosy _____

Punctuation tools

Style guide for writing a film review

Magazines, websites and newspapers all have specific styles that their writers must follow.

A style guide is a set of guidelines for writing and presentation including information about the following:

- word limits
- acceptable spellings
- punctuation
- presentation matters including font size, when to use italics, etc.

1 Reread the **film review** to answer the following questions. These will help you create your own style guide for writing a film review.

a Which words are written using *italics*?

....

b How is the release date (year) of a film written?

....

c Where and how are actors' names written in the review?

....

....

d Is the review a factual report? Give examples.

....

....

e What is the approximate word count of the review?

....

2 Complete the following table by writing numbers 1–8 to show the order of the content in the review. The second one has been done for you.

Review content	Order of content
Characters' names/actors' names	
Title of film, director's name, release date	1
Reviewer's personal response	
Plot	
Genre, background, history	
Film techniques	
Themes/messages	
Reviewer's name	

Pseudonym, pen name or nom de plume

Many writers do not use their own name when writing. They may adopt a pseudonym for a variety of reasons, including not wanting potential readers to know whether they are male or female, attempting to write a different genre or not wanting anyone to know their nationality.

The reviewer's name 'P. Snow' is a pen name. The writer's real name is Timothy Semmens. His pen name is a combination of the character, 'Peeta' and the surname of the evil President 'Snow'.

A recent example of a pseudonym is by J.K. Rowling who wrote the famous *Harry Potter* series. She wrote an adult novel using the pseudonym, Robert Galbraith. It became a bestseller after the public discovered her real identity.

3 Research and complete the table by matching the real names to their corresponding pseudonyms.

George Orwell   Lewis Carroll   Mrs Silence Dogood   Dr Seuss   Lemony Snicket
Stephen King   C.S. Lewis   Mary Westmacott   Charlotte Bronte   Mark Twain

Real name	Pseudonym
a Daniel Handler	
b Theodor Seuss Geisel	
c Clive Hamilton	
d Agatha Christie	
e Benjamin Franklin	
f Charlotte Bronte	
g Reverend Charles Lutwidge Dodson	
h Samuel Longhorne Clemens	
i Eric Arthur Blair	
j Stephen King	

4 Create your own pseudonym for writing film reviews using the following steps.

a Think of your favourite film, e.g. *Batman Rises*

b Choose a first name of a character you like, e.g. Bruce as in Bruce Wayne

c Create a surname using a location in the film or key word from the title, e.g. Bruce Gotham

....

....

....

5 Many writers choose pseudonyms that do not reveal their gender. Why do you think they do this? e.g. Sam McQueen.

....

Writing and creating tools

Writing task

Write a film review of a film you have seen recently. Use a pseudonym or pen name (not your real name). You are writing for a fictional magazine called *Latest, Greatest Movies*. Your review should be 200 words.

1 **Research** – Choose a film you know well. Write notes about this film using what you have learned in Vocabulary tools (p. 85) and Punctuation tools (p. 89). Record the following information:

- title, director, release date

- genre, background, history

- outline of the plot

- characters' and actors' names

- themes/messages

- film techniques

- personal response to the film.

2 **Plan** – Decide the order in which your information will appear in your review. Be sure also to include your personal response to the film. Why do you think it is great? Why do you think it isn't great? Use examples from the film to support your point of view.

3 **Draft** – Write your film review using the correct style.

4 **Edit and proofread** – Check that you have followed the guidelines for writing a film review. Read your review. Does it tell the reader both what the film is about and what your point of view is?

Creating task

Explore **multimodal presentation methods** for your film review.

- Create a 1–2-minute podcast film review.

- Start your own **online film blog** where you can upload/post your own film reviews whenever you like.

Listen and respond to what other students have done.

- Imagine you are a film reviewer on a radio station and read your film review to the class.

- Take a survey of the class after the film reviews have been presented and compile a top 10 film list.

- **Reflect on** the language used by your classmates in one of their film reviews. In what ways has the language helped influence your opinion of the film?

Unit  8

Literary texts: First–person narratives

Tools in this unit

- Reading tools: Understanding *The Rage of Sheep*
- Grammar tools: Personal and possessive pronouns
- Vocabulary tools: Narrative conventions
- Spelling tools: Silent letters at the beginning of a word – 'k', 'w', 'h'
- Punctuation tools: Apostrophes
- Writing and creating tools: Write a narrative in the first person

Modes covered

- Receptive: Reading, listening and viewing
- Productive: Speaking, writing and creating

General capabilities

- Literacy
- Information and communication technology capability
- Critical and creative thinking

Curriculum content in this unit

- Text structure and organisation: ACELA1543, ACELA1766, ACELA1544
- Expressing and developing ideas: ACELA1547, ACELA1549
- Responding to literature: ACELT1627
- Examining literature: ACELT1629, ACELT1767
- Interacting with others: ACELY1808, ACELY1731
- Interpreting, analysing, evaluating: ACELY1733, ACELY1734
- Creating texts: ACELY1736, ACELY1810, ACELY1738

Responding to texts

The Rage of Sheep by Michelle Cooper (2007)

'Well, all right, she does have an accent,' I said. 'But *everyone* has an accent.'

'Excuse me, I don't have an accent,' said Natalie. 'And Lynda doesn't either. You . . .' She considered for a whole *insulting* second. 'You don't. But your mum does. Of course she does. She's a . . . she's *foreign*.'

'We *all* have Australian accents,' I said, my voice wavering. I *hated* when that happened! It made me sound scared instead of furious! I took a deep breath. 'And my mother speaks English *perfectly well*.'

'Will you two stop it?' said Lynda, still searching for her timetable. 'Hester, it doesn't matter anyway, it just means she hasn't been speaking English as long as . . . Oh, here it is.'

I restrained the urge to snatch Lynda's diary out of her hand and smack her across the face with it. 'My mother,' I said, 'has been speaking English twenty years longer than you have and her vocabulary is ten times the size of yours! And to answer your question, you have Home Economics now, Natalie has Commerce and I have Advanced Mathematics, the way we do every second Wednesday. I'll see you both at Assembly.' I spun on one heel and stormed off, almost knocking over Mr Everett, who was lugging his chair back to the staffroom.

Source: Cooper, M. 2007, *The Rage of Sheep*, Random House, Sydney, p. 46.

Understanding *The Rage of Sheep*

Read the extract from **The Rage of Sheep** and answer the following questions. You may use a dictionary.

1 List the five characters in the extract.

....

2 Who are arguing and what are they arguing about?

....

....

....

3 From whose point of view is this story being told?

....

4 Why is Hester so angry? How do you know?

....

....

....

5 How does the author emphasise certain words in the extract?

....

6 Tick one box only for each of the following questions.

a The author uses ellipses (. . .) to show:

pauses in speech ❑

missing words ❑

swearing ❑

b Hester is:

proud of her mother's English ❑

embarrassed by her mother's English ❑

untruthful about her mother's English ❑

c The author's message in this scene is:

that you can still speak English well with an accent ❑

that you can't speak English well with an accent ❑

that you can't speak English well without an accent ❑

Personal and possessive pronouns

A personal pronoun can replace a noun when that noun has already been used in a sentence.

Example: '**Hester**' can be replaced with '**she**'.

Personal pronouns relate to the 'person' or perspective from which a story is told. For example, *The Rage of Sheep* is a **first-person narrative** or Hester's story told from her perspective, distinguished by her use of pronouns such as '**I**', '**me**', '**my**' and '**mine**'.

Be sure to always replace a noun with a pronoun of the same gender, number and person.

Possessive pronouns refer to items that belong to people and show ownership. They can be either **singular** or **plural**.

Example: '**Hester's book**' can be replaced with '**her book**'.

Person	Singular	Plural
First person	I my mine	our ours
Second person	yours	your yours
Third person	her its his	their theirs

1 List the two different personal pronouns in the first paragraph of the extract.

2 Write the names of the characters that the following pronouns from paragraph three refer to.

a we ....

b me ....

c I ....

d my ....

3 Complete the following table using pronouns from paragraph five of the extract.

Pronoun	Person or item referred to	Personal/possessive Singular/plural
I	Hester	personal, singular
her		
my		
you		
your		
we		
his		

4 Cross out words and write the correct pronoun above the word in the following extracts so that they are written in the first person and use correct pronouns.

a **Colin's first day in Oz**

Mum and Colin stepped out of the airport. Colin had a conversation with dad on the way to their

new house. When Colin, mum and dad arrived at the house, Colin was unable to hide Colin's

disappointment. Colin could not compare this ghetto with the luxurious mansion Colin and his

mum had in Northern China...

b Ouija board

… Suddenly a sharp pain shot up Gus' arm and Gus gave out a small gasp, before realising

that the glass had started to move. Gus examined this unbelievable act as Gus saw all fingers

positioned almost 90 degrees from the top of the glass. Gus' heart beat fast in disbelief…

c When Death Comes

…Lucas felt sick, Lucas couldn't breathe and Lucas' heart was pounding, threatening to tear a

hole in Lucas' chest. Lucas thought that perhaps someone had broken into the house, or that

Lucas' sister had broken a bone or something but this was much worse than Lucas expected…

Narrative conventions

Narratives tell a story. A narrative can be any length from micro fiction (25 words) to a whopping 1000-page novel. Narratives include novels, short stories, fairy tales, folk tales, film scripts, longer poems such as ballads, non-fiction texts and graphic novels.

Narratives are written for different purposes – to entertain, to inform, to amuse or to educate. They may combine text with images, or may use only images to tell a story (see Unit 10).

Regardless of these differences, most narratives have similar features or elements (see Unit 5, p. 57 for details) that shape the plot and action.

Most narratives follow the three-point story format:

1 **Introduction** – where the characters and setting are introduced and a problem or conflict appears

2 **Middle** – where the story advances and obstacles or more conflict impact on the character/s

3 **End** – usually where the problem is resolved and there is some growth or change in the character/s.

1 The extract from **The Rage of Sheep** is from the middle of the narrative. Can you identify from this extract what you think one of the main points of conflict is in this book? Provide quotations to support your ideas.

```
------------------------------------------------------------
------------------------------------------------------------
------------------------------------------------------------
------------------------------------------------------------
------------------------------------------------------------
------------------------------------------------------------
```

✂ Spelling tools 🖊

Silent letters at the beginning of a word – 'k', 'w', 'h'

1 When the letter 'k' starts a word and is followed by 'n', the **'k' is silent** (you don't sound it).

Examples: knee, kneel, knitting, knight, knock, knots, know, knuckle

2 When the letter 'w' starts a word and is followed by 'r', the **'w' is silent**.

Examples: wrong, write, wrinkle, wrist, wreak, wreck, wrestle, wriggle, wrap

3 When the letter 'r' starts a word and is followed by 'h', the **'h' is silent**.

Examples: rhinoceros, rhubarb, rhythm, rhyme, rheumatic

1 Underline the spelling mistakes in 'Sam's school rules' and write the correct spellings in the spaces provided.

Sam's school rules

a Nock before entering class (or Ms Gonzo will go nuts). _____

b Always rap stinky sandwiches in plastic (peeuuu!) _____

c Don't get caught restling in the yard (automatic detention). _____

d Avoid the nuckles of the school bully (they hurt big time). _____

e Always rite name on the late list at reception. _____

f Neel in chapel (Mr Ross at the back always checks). _____

g Swearing in class is rong.com! _____

h Never ever say that Miss Fimiani has rinkles (if you want to pass Italian).

_____

i Rinoceros is ALWAYS in the Y8 spelling bee. _____

j Don't riggle in Inspector Bain's classes. _____

2 Underline the nine spelling mistakes in this letter and write the correct spellings in the space provided.

Mr Everett

I no you love English class but I hate riting essays. It hurts my rist and I always spell words rongly. Besides, when I rite a poem I can't make it ryme and it just recks the poem the more I try to do it. I would rather rite about my favourite fruit, rubarb.

Hester

_____

_____

Punctuation tools

Apostrophes

Apostrophes in contractions

Contractions are words in which letters have been omitted or left out.

Apostrophes are used to indicate the missing letters and to show that the word is now in its abbreviated or shorter form.

Examples: do not = don't   we are = we're   you are = you're

Apostrophes of possession

Apostrophes are also used to show that one thing belongs to another.

Example: Hester's new cat is black. (The cat belongs to Hester.)

While apostrophes are usually added before the 's', this is not always the case:

- If there is more than one person to whom the thing belongs, the apostrophe must be placed *after* the 's'.

Example: All of the girls' dresses at the school dance were lovely. (The dresses belonged to all the girls.)

- If the noun already ends with an 's', you can place the apostrophe *after* the 's'.

Example: Hester went to Chris' house for dinner on Monday. (The house belongs to Chris.)

Contractions should not be used in formal writing such as essays.

1 Rewrite the following sentences changing the full word into its contracted form.

a Hester has not eaten lunch yet.

....

b The school bell should have rung five minutes ago.

....

c They are all going to Natalie's party on Saturday.

....

d Lynda is not happy with the mark Mr Everett gave her for her book report.

....

....

2 Rewrite the following using apostrophes to show possession. The first has been done for you.

a the timetable of Caroline   *Caroline's timetable*

b the score of the team ....

c the mother of Hester ....

d the lunches of the students ....

e the office of the principal ....

Writing and creating tools

Writing task 1

Choose a topic from the box below and write a 250-word narrative in the first person. Use the correct personal and possessive pronouns. Your audience is your class.

a bad day at school   a birthday party   a teacher you like   a problem you have had

1 **Research** – Choose your topic. This is a personal piece; what do you want to say about this topic? Write sentences with correct personal pronouns. Write descriptions with the correct possessive pronouns.

2 **Plan** – Consider how you will structure your narrative: Introduction, Middle and End. Was there an obstacle you overcame? In what style will you write your narrative?

3 **Draft** – Write a draft of your first-person narrative.

4 **Edit and proofread** – Read over your narrative. Check your spelling and punctuation. Make sure you have used personal and possessive pronouns correctly. Check that you have used apostrophes correctly.

Listen and respond to what other students have done.

- Read your **first-person narrative** to the class as an **oral presentation**.

- In small groups discuss how the narrative may have a different effect on the audience if it is written in the second or third person.

- Swap first-person narratives with a classmate. Change the order of the narrative's events. Comment on how this affects the reader. For example, is it more or less interesting? Why?

Writing task 2

Follow the same steps as above and **rewrite** your first-person narrative in either the **second** or the **third person**. Change the conventional order of events in your narrative – for example, consider starting your narrative at the end, or putting the conflict/obstacle first.

Revision tools: Units 5–8

Complete these questions by yourself. You may use a dictionary.

Grammar tools

Darshan and documentaries

Darshan never watched documentaries because he wrongly thought they were boring. Recently, he saw the documentary called *Chicken Rescue* and he was instantly hooked! His sister wisely advised him about all the Australian documentaries she had seen and lent Darshan her copy of *Cane Toads*. 'I want to become a documentary filmmaker!' he declared.

Read the text above and then answer the following.

1 What tense is the text written in? ....

2 Rewrite the first sentence in the present tense. You need to change three verbs.

....

....

3 Write three adverbs of time used in the text.

....

....

4 Write two adverbs of manner used in the text.

....

....

Spelling tools

5 Underline the 10 incorrectly spelt words in 'Documentary funding' and write the correct versions in the space provided.

Documentary funding

Darshan began filming an enviromental documentary about plastic bags. In the begining he rongly thought that he would rite and request goverment funding. He was hopeing for $10 000 so he could create a styleish and carefuly made film. Unfortunatly the government rejected his application because he was only 14 years old. Darshan learnt from his expeirience and asked his older brother to apply.

....

....

....

....

Punctuation tools

6 Write the contracted forms of the following.

a cannot ....

b I have ....

c who is ....

d you are ....

e he will ....

f I would ....

7 Write the complete versions of the following.

a won't ....

b she's ....

c it's ....

d you're ....

e we'd ....

f there's ....

Unit 9

Literary texts: Poetry

Tools in this unit

- Reading tools: Understanding 'Mushrooms'
- Grammar tools: Recap – Adjectives
- Vocabulary tools: Poetic terms and techniques
- Spelling tools: Poetry spelling list
- Punctuation tools: Writing free verse poetry
- Writing and creating tools: Write a two-stanza free verse poem

Modes covered

- Receptive: Reading, listening and viewing
- Productive: Speaking, writing and creating

General capabilities

- Literacy
- Personal and social capability
- Information and communication technology capability
- Critical and creative thinking

Curriculum content in this unit

- Language for interaction: ACELA1542
- Text structure and organisation: ACELA1543, ACELA1809
- Expressing and developing ideas: ACELA1547, ACELA1549
- Literature and context: ACELT1626
- Responding to literature: ACELT1627
- Examining literature: ACELT1629, ACELT1630, ACELT1767
- Interacting with others: ACELY1808, ACELY1731
- Interpreting, analysing, evaluating: ACELY1732
- Creating texts: ACELY1736, ACELY1810, ACELEY1738

Responding to texts

'Mushrooms' by Sylvia Plath (1960)

Overnight, very
Whitely, discreetly,
Very quietly

Our toes, our noses
Take hold on the loam,
Acquire the air.

Nobody sees us,
Stops us, betrays us;
The small grains make room.

Soft fists insist on
Heaving the needles,
The leafy bedding,

Even the paving.
Our hammers, our rams.
Earless and eyeless,

Perfectly voiceless,
Widen the crannies,
Shoulder through holes. We

Diet on water,
On crumbs of shadow,
Bland-mannered, asking

Little or nothing.
So many of us!
So many of us!

We are shelves, we are
Tables, we are meek,
We are edible,

Nudgers and shovers
In spite of ourselves.
Our kind multiplies:

We shall by morning
Inherit the earth.
Our foot's in the door.

Source: Plath, Sylvia, 'Mushrooms' (1981), *Collected Poems*, Faber and Faber, UK, pp. 65–6.

Understanding 'Mushrooms'

Read **'Mushrooms'** aloud and then answer the following questions. You may use a dictionary.

1 Who or what is speaking in this poem?

....

2 List the words the poet uses to give the mushrooms human characteristics.

....

....

3 List the actions that the mushrooms take that give them human characteristics.

....

....

....

....

4 Why does nobody see the mushrooms?

....

....

....

....

5 How does the poet describe the soil the mushrooms grow in? ....

....

6 What do the mushrooms feed on? ....

....

7 Define the word 'loam'. ....

....

8 Why do the mushrooms have to be 'nudgers' and 'shovers'? What does this description tell you about them?

....

....

....

....

9 What is the effect of repeating the line 'So many of us!' in the eleventh stanza?

....

....

....

....

Grammar tools

Recap – Adjectives

Adjectives are **describing words**. Specifically, they **describe nouns and pronouns**, or people, places, things, feelings and experiences. Adjectives **tell us something more** about the **quality** of the noun or pronoun being used. Adjectives can help the reader to imagine the characters and places that you describe by creating pictures in their minds.

For example, you might write a simple sentence like this:

The cat has a black coat.

However, adding more adjectives to your sentence to describe the nouns ('cat' and 'coat') helps to create a more vivid picture of the cat.

For example: The cat has a **shiny, gleaming black** coat.

1 Identify the adjectives used to describe the following nouns in the poem **'Mushrooms'**.

a grains _____

b fists _____

c bedding _____

d manners _____

2 The following sentences are missing adjectives. Place descriptive words of your choice in the spaces provided.

a The children next door are afraid of the _____ old woman.

b It was a _____ Sunday because it was too hot to go outside.

c The wind blew _____ and _____ throughout the garden.

d I can see the _____ mountain at the end of the _____ road.

3 Write as many adjectives as you can to describe the following image of a winter landscape.

Vocabulary tools

Poetic terms and techniques

Poems tell stories. Poems are organised into stanzas (paragraphs) and use poetic techniques such as descriptive language, as well as many of the rules of grammar you have learned in this workbook.

Poems differ from prose in that they rely on two major techniques: **imagery** (creating pictures with words) and **sound devices** (things we hear when we read).

A list of poetic terms and techniques is provided below.

Alliteration
A sound device that uses words starting with the same sound for emphasis or effect.
Example: **clever, curious cat**

Assonance
A sound device that repeats vowel sounds in words placed close together.
Example: **The clown drowned his crown.**

Metaphor
An imagery technique by which poets describe or compare something or someone by directly saying that it is something else.
Example: Her heart **is** gold (meaning she is a kind-hearted person).

Onomatopoeia
A sound device using words and phrases that sound like the things they are describing.
Examples: **hiss, pop, splash, fizz**

Personification
An imagery technique similar to metaphor that gives human characteristics to something not human.
Example: **weeping willow**

Rhyme
A sound device that uses words that finish with the same sound.
Example: '**tale**' rhymes with '**sale**'.

Simile
An imagery technique by which poets describe or create images by comparing two things using the words '**like**' and/or '**as**'.
Example: His fearful eyes were round **like** saucers.

Symbol/ symbolism
A word or reference that represents or stands for something else.
Example: A dove is a symbol of peace.

1 How many stanzas are there in **'Mushrooms'**? ....

2 Identify three examples of assonance in the poem.

....

....

....

....

3 Identify two examples of metaphors in the poem.

....

....

4 Create your own metaphors from the prompts below.

a .... is a rose.

b The sun is a ....

c .... is a long road.

d Happiness is a ....?

5 Imagine it is raining outside your window. Write five onomatopoeic words that describe the sound the rain makes.

....

....

6 'Mushrooms' is an excellent example of personification sustained throughout a whole poem. Write examples of personification using the following objects. For example: *My computer has died.*

a mobile phone

b television

c bicycle

d breeze

e branch

f homework

7 'Mushrooms' features lovely examples of alliteration, such as **'Soft fists insist'**. Write your own examples of alliteration using the following words. For example: *clever, curious cat*

a sister

b dog

c book

d moon ....

....

e tree ....

....

8 Each poem has countless possible interpretations. Read **'Mushrooms'** again and consider that the mushrooms are a symbol in the poem for something else. What do you think they might be a symbol of? Write a short paragraph justifying your point of view.

....

....

....

....

....

....

Spelling tools

Poetry spelling list

Poems are made up of descriptive language and often use difficult words whose meaning might not be immediately known to you. When you read a poem it is a good tip to keep a list of the words you don't immediately understand and use a dictionary to look them up. Then read the poem again. Knowing the word's correct meaning will enhance your understanding and appreciation of the poem. Spelling the word correctly is also important.

1 Use a dictionary and write definitions of the following words from **'Mushrooms'**.

a discreetly ....

....

b acquire ....

....

c heaving ....

....

d rams ....

....

e crannies ....

....

f shoulder ....

....

g bland ....

....

h meek ....

....

⚒ Punctuation tools

Writing free verse poetry

Free verse poetry is a style of poetry that does not use a regular metric pattern. Despite the fact that free poetry does not rhyme, does not have regular line lengths and does not use much punctuation, there is still a recognisable rhythmic pattern. Most free verse poetry creates its own logic and rules.

1 Answer the following about how punctuation is used in **'Mushrooms'**.

a How many lines are there in the poem? ....

b How many lines are there in every stanza? ....

c Which punctuation symbol is used most frequently in the poem? ....

d In addition to commas, which punctuation symbols are frequently used and what is their effect when reading?

....

....

e Why do you think the word 'We' is located at the end of the 6th stanza rather than the beginning of the 7th?

....

2 Choose one of the following words and use it as a starting point to write freely, without punctuation for two minutes.

snow   running   escape   cherries   curtains   October   horses   ice   feathers

✂ Writing and creating tools

Writing task

Choose one of the four images on this and the following page and write a two-stanza free verse poem. Your poem should include two similes and two metaphors. Use at least 10 different adjectives. Include an example of alliteration. Your poem does not have to be specifically about the image but can be about whatever the image inspires you to think of. It can be an emotion or a memory or something else.

1 **Research** – Use a dictionary or thesaurus to help you find a variety of words to describe what you see and feel. Experiment with writing similes and metaphors to build your free verse poem around.

2 **Plan** – Make a list of the 10 adjectives you will use in your poem. Decide on what information you will put in each stanza.

3 **Draft** – Write your free verse poem. Rework your similes and metaphors if needed.

4 **Edit and proofread** – Read over your poem. Check that you have used 10 adjectives and that your similes and metaphors make sense.

Creating task

Explore **multimodal presentation methods** for poetry.

- Broadcast yourself reading the free verse poem with a **podcast**.

- Create a **storyboard** for your stanza or poem – one image per line.

Listen and respond to what other students have done.

- Read your finished poem to the class as an **oral presentation**; then explain what inspired you to write what you have and how you thought of your similes and metaphors.

- Write a 50-word summary of one of the oral presentations and identify the poetic techniques.

Unit

Visual texts: Graphic novels

Tools in this unit

- Reading tools: Understanding *The Arrival*
- Grammar tools: Past participles
- Vocabulary tools: Visual vocabulary
- Spelling tools: Visual grammar spelling list
- Punctuation tools: Sentences
- Writing and creating tools: Write your own text for *The Arrival*

Modes covered

- Receptive: Reading, listening and viewing
- Productive: Speaking, writing and creating

General capabilities

- Literacy
- Personal and social capability
- Information and communication technology capability
- Critical and creative thinking
- Ethical understanding

Curriculum content in this unit

- Language for interaction: ACELA1541
- Text structure and organisation: ACELA1543
- Expressing and developing ideas: ACELA1548, ACELA1547
- Responding to literature: ACELT1628
- Examining literature: ACELT1629, ACELT1767
- Creating literature: ACELT1632, ACELT1768
- Interacting with others: ACELY1808, ACELY1731
- Interpreting, analysing, evaluating: ACELY1732, ACELY1734, ACELY1735
- Creating texts: ACELY1736, ACELY1810, ACELY1738

Responding to texts

The Arrival by Shaun Tan (2006)

Source: Tan, S. 2006, *The Arrival*, Lothian, Sydney, pp. 8–9.

Understanding *The Arrival*

Study the extract from **The Arrival**, then answer the following questions. You may use a dictionary.

1 What common text element is missing from this extract?

....

2 What do you think is happening in this extract?

....

....

3 What do you think the relationship between these characters is?

....

....

4 How do these images make you feel?

....

....

5 What type of text is this extract from **The Arrival**? Tick one box.

a speech ❑

a graphic novel ❑

a picture book ❑

Grammar tools

Past participles

A **participle** combines with an auxiliary verb to form a compound verb. There are two types of participles: past and present (see Unit 12, p. 155).

Past participles are formed by adding 'ed' to regular verbs; they indicate that an action took place in the past.

Example: study + ed = studied

The past participle combines with an auxiliary verb to form a complete (compound) verb.

Example: had studied

Some irregular verbs end in 't' or 'n'. Other verbs do not change their endings.

Example: hurt, cut, let

Fix it!

What's the difference between a past tense verb and a past participle?

Past participle + auxiliary verb will make sense. *Example:* 'have seen'

Past tense + auxiliary verb won't make sense. *Example:* 'have saw'

1   Rewrite the following verbs as past participles.

a   take _____

b   achieve _____

c   improve _____

d   focus _____

e assist ....

f benefit ....

2 Complete the following table of **irregular verbs**. These past participles do not end in 'ed'. The first line has been completed for you.

Irregular verb	Past participle
begin	begun
forget	
give	
see	
ride	
make	
hurt	
let	
know	

Vocabulary tools

Visual vocabulary

Visual texts include graphic novels, like *The Arrival*, picture books, films, TV shows, photographs and advertisements.

To be able to speak and write confidently about visual texts you need to build up a **visual vocabulary**. There are certain features you should pay particular attention to when talking about visual texts.

Features	Questions to ask when reading or viewing
Composition of image	How are images within the text positioned?
Setting and location	Where is the text set? Is there anything interesting or unusual about the location chosen by the author? Is the setting symbolic? (Does it represent something else?)
Characters	Is one character central to the text? How do you know this? How do characters in the text look and speak (if moving images are used)? What do we learn about a character from their clothing?
Angles or framing	Where are characters positioned within the frame of the image and in relation to other characters? Are characters represented as equals? Are characters viewed at eye level, low level or high level? Are they viewed in close-up? Whose point of view is being represented?
Juxtaposition	How are images within the text put together or contrasted? What does this tell you about the story?
Colour and lighting	How is colour used within the text? What feelings do colours evoke? For example, dark colours may suggest a sense of dread or mystery, whereas yellow may suggest happiness or joy. How do shadows create atmosphere?

Mood and feeling	Describe the atmosphere of the text. What feeling does it evoke in the reader? How do details like colour and light affect this?
Symbols	Do any elements recur throughout the text that have 'symbolic' meaning to the text as a whole, e.g. a black cat representing danger or magic, or a red rose representing love?

1   Who are the characters in this extract from **The Arrival**? How are they positioned within the image panels?

....

....

....

....

....

2   How is colour used in **The Arrival**? What impact does this have on how you think about the story?

....

....

....

....

3   Is there an element that recurs in these images that might be understood as symbolic? What do you think it might mean or represent?

....

----

4 Describe the setting in this extract from *The Arrival*.

----

5 Choose one character and briefly describe the angles and framing used to present that character.

Spelling tools

Visual grammar spelling list

| contrasted | audience | mysterious | inspires | promotes | symbolic |

1 Find a word in the box above to complete each of the following sentences. The words will all help you to describe your response to a visual text. You should learn to spell them correctly. Use a dictionary to help you understand the words.

a The intended _____ for this text is teenage girls.

b Colour in the text is dark and creates a _____ atmosphere.

c The image of the dog in the text is _____ with the image of the bird.

d The man's hat is _____ of the journey he is taking.

e The text _____ feelings of joy.

f The text _____ an understanding of how other people live.

2 Write a brief story of **The Arrival** in your own words. Include characters, setting and mood.

_____

_____

_____

_____

_____

_____

3 Use three of the words from the box in question 1 in three separate sentences that describe your response to the extract from *The Arrival*.

_____

_____

_____

_____

_____

_____

_____

_____

Punctuation tools

Sentences

A sentence:

- is a group of words containing a **subject** and at least one verb (or **predicate**: see Unit 5, p. 55)

- makes sense on its own

- always begins with a capital letter

- ends with either a full stop, a question mark or an exclamation mark.

There are four main types of sentences:

1 Command – an order or very strong instruction

Example: Do not touch the hot plate!

2 Question – a sentence that asks something or seeks information

Example: Why are you still awake at this late hour?

3 Statement – a sentence that states a fact or opinion

Example: It was a sunny afternoon and Joanna sat in the park and read a book.

4 Exclamation – A sentence that ends suddenly, expresses shock or surprise or other strong feelings

Example: I love you!

1 What types of sentences are these? Identify and write your answer in the space provided.

a There are four bananas left in the fruit bowl.

....

b Stop talking! ....

c Michael ran after the bus. ....

d What would you like to eat for dinner tonight?

....

e I can't believe you just said that! _____

2 Underline the verbs and circle the subjects in the following sentences.

a I am walking our dog, Rex.

b We celebrate Nanna's birthday with a big party every year.

c Sean misunderstood what the teacher was asking him to do.

d How can we get to school on time when the bus has broken down again?

Remember:

To find the subject of a sentence you must first find the verb, then ask: *who* or *what* performed the action indicated by the verb?

Example: Ben was eating an apple.

verb: was eating

Who or *what* was eating? Ben was; therefore 'Ben' is the **subject**.

---

3 Write three sentences, each with a different subject and verb, using the image on p. 136.

Underline the different verbs and circle the different subjects.

_____

_____

_____

_____

_____

_____

🛠 Writing and creating tools

Writing task

The panels of the extract from **The Arrival** tell a story without using words. Many other graphic novels combine words and images to construct their narratives. Write text for these panels – one or two sentences each – either to describe what is happening, or to provide dialogue for one or all of the characters. Use a variety of sentences.

1 **Research** – Make notes in your own workbook about what you think is happening in the extract, and then notes for what you think is happening in each of the panels. What is the story being told?

2 **Plan** – Number the panels and number your sentences so they match. Give the characters names if you wish. Think about the things these characters might want to say to each other. How does the overall composition of the images influence your understanding of the action? What does the use of colour and light tell you about the mood of these events? Consider how you might write about any symbolic images.

3 **Draft** – Write your sentences so that they correspond to the action in the panels.

4 **Edit and proofread** – Read over your text. Have you used a variety of sentences? Check spelling and punctuation. While this is only a short extract from a longer graphic novel, these panels do tell a compelling story. Have your words made this story more exciting?

Creating task

Explore **multimodal presentation methods** for your visual text.

- Write the script for an interview between you and one of the three key characters in the extract. Write six key questions and the answers to them. Choose a partner to play the role of the character. Record the interview, either as a **podcast** or, if you have access to a **digital video camera**, as a video clip.

- If you have access to the free downloadable program Microsoft Photo Story 3, use it to turn your interview into a **digital story** with text and images.

Listen and respond to what other students have done.

- In pairs, perform your interview as an **oral presentation** to the class.

- Listen to the interviews and list the different information revealed about the characters. Write a list of any extra questions you would like to ask the characters.

Unit  11

Literary texts: Dialogue

Tools in this unit

- Reading tools: Understanding *A Study in Scarlet*
- Grammar tools: Recap – Adjectives of degree
- Vocabulary tools: Homophones and homonyms
- Spelling tools: Number prefixes
- Punctuation tools: Direct and indirect speech
- Writing and creating tools: Write a descriptive dialogue

Modes covered

- Receptive: Listening and reading
- Productive: Speaking, writing and creating

General capabilities

- Literacy
- Information and communication technology capability
- Critical and creative thinking
- Numeracy

Curriculum content in this unit

- Text structure and organisation: ACELA1766, ACELA1809
- Expressing and developing ideas: ACELA1547, ACELA1549
- Responding to literature: ACELT1627
- Examining literature: ACELT1629, ACELT1767
- Creating literature: ACELT1632, ACELT1768
- Interacting with others: ACELY1730, ACELY1808, ACELY1731
- Creating texts: ACELY1736, ACELY1810, ACELY1738

Responding to texts

A *Study in Scarlet* by Sir Arthur Conan Doyle (1887)

'Come along, Doctor,' he said; 'we shall go and look him up. I'll tell you one thing which may help you in the case,' he continued, turning to the two detectives. 'There has been murder done, and the murderer was a man. He was more than six feet high, was in the prime of life, had small feet for his height, wore coarse, square-toed boots and smoked a Trichinopoly cigar. He came here with his victim in a four-wheeled cab, which was drawn by a horse with three old shoes and one new one on his off fore-leg. In all probability the murderer had a florid face, and the finger-nails of his right hand were remarkably long. These are only a few indications, but they may assist you.'

Lestrade and Gregson glanced at each other with an incredulous smile.

'If this man was murdered, how was it done?' asked the former.

'Poison,' said Sherlock Holmes curtly, and strode off. 'One other thing, Lestrade,' he added, turning around at the door: '"Rache" is the German word for "revenge"; so don't lose your time looking for Miss Rachel.'

With which Parthian shot he walked away, leaving the two rivals open-mouthed behind him.

Source: Conan Doyle, Arthur, 1887, *A Study in Scarlet*, Ward Lock & Co, United Kingdom.

Reading tools

Understanding A *Study in Scarlet*

Read the extract from **A Study in Scarlet**, then answer the following questions. You may use a dictionary.

1 Who is the author of this extract? In what year was it first published?

....

2 List the names of the four different characters in the extract.

....

3 What five pieces of information does Holmes reveal about the murderer's appearance?

....

....

....

4 According to Holmes, what killed the victim?

....

5 Why might the detectives be looking for a Miss Rachel?

....

....

....

6 List four things you learn about Sherlock Holmes from the extract.

7 Write brief definitions for the following words:

incredulous

florid

fore-leg

victim

8 What is a Parthian shot?

Grammar tools

Recap – Adjectives of degree

Adjectives can tell to what degree (or extent) a noun or pronoun is being described.

There are three degrees of adjectives: **positive**, **comparative** and **superlative**.

Positive (describes one noun)	Comparative (compares two nouns)	Superlative (compares more than two nouns)
Sam had a **long** sleep.	Sam had the **longer** sleep.	Sam had the **longest** sleep.
beautiful	more beautiful	most beautiful
many	more	most
bad	worse	worst
good	better	best
lazy	lazier	laziest

1   Answer the following questions using adjectives from the extract.

a   What size were the murderer's feet? _____

b   What was the horse's last-mentioned shoe like? _____

c   What was the face of the murderer like? _____

d   What were the fingernails on his right hand like? _____

2   Underline the incorrect adjective in each of the following sentences.

a   Sherlock Holmes is the (cleverer/cleverest) character in the story.

b   Holmes is (smarter/smartest) than the two detectives.

c   Please hold the (thinnest/thinner) end of the rope.

3 Complete the following adjective table.

Positive	Comparative	Superlative
cautious		
	more handsome	
		worst
old		
	smaller	

Vocabulary tools

Homophones and homonyms

A **homophone** is a word that is pronounced the same as another word but has a different spelling and different meaning.

Here are some common homophones:

one – won	night – knight
meet – meat	sole – soul
whole – hole	see – sea

A **homonym** is a word that is spelt one way but has multiple, different meanings.

Here are some common homonyms:

soil	bank	bill	dear	row	wave

1 Write brief definitions for the following homophones.

a pause _____

_____

   paws _____

_____

b course _____

_____

_____

_____

   coarse _____

_____

c road _____

_____

   rode _____

d night _____

   knight _____

e sole _____

   soul _____

f whole _____

   hole _____

2 Write two definitions for the following homonyms and state which part of speech each one is (e.g. noun, verb, adjective).

a bear

b grave

c implement

d bank

e wave

3 Write homophones and their meanings for the following.

a wave ....

b metal ....

Spelling tools

Number prefixes

Some prefixes are explicitly associated with numbers and are added to the beginning of words to indicate quantities of things, events and measures of time.

Here are the most common number prefixes:

uni, mono (one)	pent, qui (five)	non (nine)
duo, bi (two)	sex (six)	dec (ten)
tri (three)	sept (seven)	cent (hundred)
quad, quart (four)	oct (eight)	

1 Write brief definitions of the following words and include the associated numbers.

a monocle ....

....

....

b monologue ....

....

c bicycle ....

....

d triathlon ....

....

....

2 Write the words with number prefixes that match the following definitions.

a period of 10 years ....

b mythical animal with one horn ....

c five-pointed star ....

d one of a kind ....

e able to speak two languages with ease ....

f an athletics contest with seven different types of events ....

Direct and indirect speech

Direct speech represents the exact words spoken by someone. This is shown in written texts by using quotation marks at the beginning and end of the actual words spoken.

Example: 'See you tomorrow, Holmes.'

Indirect speech (or reported speech) describes what the speaker has said. It does not use the actual words and therefore does not require quotation marks.

Example: The murderer greeted Holmes.

Five rules for writing direct speech

1 Start a new paragraph for each new speaker.

2 There is no need to include speakers' names every time.

3 Use single quotation marks.

4 If there is a quote within direct speech, use double quotation marks for the quote.

5 Punctuation marks go inside the final quotation mark if they relate to the quoted words, but outside if they relate to the whole sentence.

Example: 'Get out of my way, you madman!' yelled Holmes.

1 Which characters speak in the extract from **A Study in Scarlet**?

....

2 Write an example from the extract of a quote within a quote. ....

....

....

3 Edit the following by adding quotation marks where necessary.

a Boy, Sherlock Holmes was a smart detective, commented Sam.

b He knew about forensic science before it was even invented, he continued. And he knew all about blood splatters.

c Sophie interrupted, You know that Sherlock Holmes is a fictional character, don't you?

d Great! exclaimed Sam, Did he have any enemies?

4 Rewrite two of the sentences above as indirect speech.

⚒ Writing and creating tools

Writing task

Imagine that you are an eyewitness to a robbery and are being interviewed by a police detective. Write a dialogue between yourself and the detective, in which you include a detailed description of the criminal's appearance. This dialogue should be 150 words.

1 **Research** – In your own workbook, make decisions about what you witnessed. What was stolen and what did the criminal look like? Consider the following: height, weight, hair colour and any other distinguishing physical features. Have you heard the criminal speak? What did they say? What were they wearing? How did they behave?

2 **Plan** – Decide what questions the detective will ask you. Number the questions in the order they will appear in the final descriptive dialogue.

3 **Draft** – Write a draft of your descriptive dialogue.

4 **Edit and proofread** – Read over your dialogue. Have you used different adjectives? Have you followed the rules for writing direct speech? Check your spelling and punctuation. Do you think you have provided enough information about the robber for the police to make an arrest?

Creating task

Explore **multimodal presentation methods** for your descriptive dialogue.

- In pairs, use a microphone or recording device to record the dialogue. One of you takes on the role of the police detective, the other the role of the eyewitness.

- Broadcast your descriptive dialogue as a **podcast**.

Listen and respond to what other students have done.

- Perform your dialogue for the class. After your performance, briefly explain why you described the criminal in this way.

- While you listen to the dialogues, sketch and label the various criminals described. Pay particular attention to the use of adjectives.

Unit

Instructional texts

Tools in this unit

- Reading tools: Understanding 'How to become a better student'
- Grammar tools: Infinitive verbs and present participles
- Vocabulary tools: Study verbs
- Spelling tools: More common prefixes
- Punctuation tools: Bullet points and full colons
- Writing and creating tools: Write a set of instructions

Modes covered

- Receptive: Listening and reading
- Productive: Speaking, writing and creating

General capabilities

- Literacy
- Personal and social capability
- Information and communication technology capability
- Critical and creative thinking

Curriculum content in this unit

- Text structure and organisation: ACELA1809
- Expressing and developing ideas: ACELA1546, ACELA1547
- Examining literature: ACELT1767
- Interacting with others: ACELY1730, ACELY1808, ACELY1731
- Interpreting, analysing, evaluating: ACELY1732, ACELY1734
- Creating texts: ACELY1736, ACELY1810, ACELY1738

Responding to texts

'How to become a better student'

I don't mean the total geek variety of organised student who has no life outside school. I just mean your average, everyday could-do-better-if-they-were-organised variety of student. The type of student everyone would like to be, if it didn't cut in to their chill time. Trust me. Better a little pain now and a lot of gain later.

Here's what you can do at home ...

Take some responsibility for your own learning. Organise a quiet study space at home and your parents will be rapt. Request a desk, proper chair (not too comfy), wall planner, highlighters and a lamp (Make sure that they aren't considered 'birthday presents'). Write the dates your assignments are due on the wall planner. Number each assignment in order of its importance. Plan to do your homework at the same time each day e.g. between 4.30 – 6.30pm. Turn your mobile to silent and place it in a cupboard.

Organise a folder for each subject and label them carefully. Think about each of your subjects and set a realistic goal that you want to achieve e.g. 75% in Maths by Term 3. Write these goals down and stick them on your wall planner so that you can see them easily. Think about how you will achieve these goals and make a list of what you need to do e.g. revise for 10 mins each night. Discuss your work with your teachers and ask for feedback e.g. how you can improve your vocabulary. Try to include some 'extra' work in each subject once a week – to get ahead.

Reward yourself when you reach a goal and make sure you let your parents know.

Reading tools

Understanding 'How to become a better student'

Read **'How to become a better student'**, then answer the following questions. You may use a dictionary.

1 What does the author mean by 'Better a little pain now and a lot of gain later'?

_____

_____

_____

2 Answer the following questions:

a What materials do you need to organise a study space at home?

_____

_____

_____

_____

b What do you need to do? _____

_____

_____

_____

_____

_____

_____

c What do you want the end result to be?

_____

_____

3 Why do you think 'feedback' from a teacher is so important?

_____

_____

4 Tick one box only for each of the following questions:

a What type of text is **'How to become a better student'**?

an essay ❑

a letter ❑

a set of instructions ❑

b Who is the intended audience for **'How to become a better student'**?

grandparents ❑

Year 5–8 students ❑

university students ❑

c The bracketed phrase '(not too comfy)' is an example of what style of writing:

descriptive ❑

science fiction ❑

humorous ❑

Grammar tools

Infinitive verbs and present participles

Infinitive verbs

An infinitive verb is a verb that cannot stand alone in a sentence. It has no reference to the subject of the sentence and often begins with the word 'to'.

Example: to clean

Participles

A participle combines with an auxiliary verb to form a compound verb. There are two types of participles: present and past (see Unit 10).

Present participles are formed by adding 'ing' to an infinitive verb.

Example: clean + ing = cleaning

The present participle combines with an auxiliary verb to form a complete (compound) verb.

Example: is cleaning

1 Rewrite six of the seven verbs in the fourth paragraph of the extract in the spaces below.

....

....

....

....

....

2 Turn the following infinitive verbs into present participles.

a (to) take _____

b (to) make _____

c (to) pick _____

d (to) tap _____

e (to) get _____

f (to) wash _____

3 Complete the following table using four of the verbs you identified in question 1.

Verb	Present participle

Vocabulary tools

Study verbs

Verbs are frequently used to explain the action you should take when responding to and answering questions. For example, when an essay prompt asks you to 'explain' something, you are being asked to do more than provide an overview of the main points.

1   Develop your vocabulary of study verbs by matching the correct study verb from the box with the definition below. You may use a dictionary.

analyse	compare	define	contrast	discuss	explain
describe	evaluate	outline	summarise	skim	scan

a   to point out similarities ....

b   to break down a topic into its main ideas and describe the relationship between them

....

c   to give reasons why a situation exists or a process occurs ....

d   to briefly provide the main points ....

e   to briefly examine the main points ....

f   to point out differences ....

g   to judge the value of something ....

h   to read a text quickly, looking for key words and phrases

....

i   to give details of something by referring to its features or characteristics

....

j   to look quickly over a text to get an idea of what it is about

....

k   to give the exact meaning ....

l   to explain the advantages and disadvantages of both sides of an issue

....

Spelling tools

More common prefixes

A **prefix** is a word or syllable placed at the beginning of a base word or root word to change its meaning. The following are some more common prefixes, their meanings and an example of each.

Prefix	Meaning	Example
arch	chief, main, highest-ranking	archbishop
hyper	too, extremely	hyperlink
hypo	under, less than normal	hypothermia
mal	badly, wrongly	malodorous
pseudo	false, pretend	pseudomorph

1   Provide one example each of words that begin with these prefixes.

a   mal ....

b   arch ....

c   hyper ....

d   pseudo ....

2   Write brief definitions or synonyms for the following words. You may use a dictionary.

a   pseudonym ....

....

b   hyperactive ....

....

c malnutrition _____

_____

d malfunction _____

e hypertension _____

f hypoglycaemia _____

_____

⚒ Punctuation tools

Bullet points and full colons

Bullet points are punctuation marks that are useful when you want to list items in your writing. Sentences in bullet points do not have to be complete or very long.

Bullet points do the following:

- send a 'must read this' signal to readers

- summarise points clearly

- use words and phrases rather than longer sentences

- start with the same part of speech, e.g. noun or verb

- have full stops at the end of each point or at the end of the last point only.

Full colon (:)

When you write bullet points you need to use a full colon at the end of the words preceding the bullet points (called a 'lead-in' line).

Example: Bullet points must do the following:

1 Rewrite the following using a lead-in line with a full colon and four bullet points.

To write an A+ essay you need the following equipment internet for research pencils and erasers for planning computer for drafting and dictionary to check your spelling.

----

2 Finish the method ('how to' steps) for cleaning your teeth using four numbered points. Numbered points follow the same rules as bullet points. You need to start each point with a verb. The first 'how to' stop has been completed for you.

How to clean your teeth

1. Squeeze a small amount of toothpaste onto your toothbrush.

Writing and creating tools

Writing task

Rewrite the extract **'How to become a better student'** as a set of clear and simple instructions for students in Years 5–8. Your instructions should not be longer than 250 words.

You need to include the following three sections:

- **Aim** (e.g. 'To become . . .')

- **Equipment** or **What you need** (using bullet points)

- **Method** (using numbered points, e.g. 1, 2, 3 . . .)

1 **Research** – Revise information about using bullet points and numbered points. Read the extract again.

2 **Plan** – Write notes for your set of instructions under the headings **Aim**, **Equipment** and **Methods** in your own workbook.

3 **Draft** – Write your instructions using bullet points and numbered points.

4 **Edit and proofread** – Read over your instructions. Are the steps in the correct order? Have you used bullet points and numbered points correctly?

Creating task

Explore **multimodal presentation methods** for your instructions.

- If you have access to a **digital camera** or a **video function on your mobile phone**, make a short film of yourself organising your quiet study space. Tip: This task is best completed in pairs, with one student filming and reading the instructions while the other performs the task.

Listen and respond to what other students have done.

- Turn your multimodal presentation into an **oral presentation** for your class.

- Write a 50-word summary of one of the presentations you have seen. Comment on whether the instructions are in the correct order.

Revision tools: Units 9–12

Complete these questions by yourself. You may use a dictionary.

Grammar tools

1 Complete the following verb table. Remember that a participle needs an auxiliary verb to make it a complete (compound) verb. Don't just write the verb in the past tense.

Verb	Past participle	Present participle
wash		
pick		
know		
give		
forget		

2 Complete the following adjective table.

Positive	Comparative	Superlative
beautiful		
	lazier	
		best
	worse	
large		

Vocabulary tools

3 Circle the incorrect homophones in the brackets for the following sentences.

a My dog had to have his (paws/pause) trimmed.

b The (guest/guessed) complained about the dog howling at night.

c We saw a (pear/pair) of shoes beside the road.

d I could see (through/threw) the window.

Spelling tools

4 Write the words from the box with their correct prefixes.

malrival   hypoactive   pseudonutrition   archnym   archform   hyperdermic

a _____

b _____

c _____

d _____

e _____

f _____

Punctuation tools

5 Rewrite the following as a list using bullet points and a full colon at the end of the lead-in line.

When you are running late home from school you should do the following call either your Mum or Dad and let them know what time you will be home try not to miss the next bus do not stop for a hamburger do not drop into Nan's house for some cake on your way.

Unit  13

Persuasive texts: Letter to the editor

Tools in this unit

- Reading tools: Understanding 'Fit for success'
- Grammar tools: Clauses
- Vocabulary tools: More persuasive language techniques
- Spelling tools: Letters that sound like 'f'
- Punctuation tools: Colons and semicolons
- Writing and creating tools: Write a formal persuasive letter

Modes covered

- Receptive: Listening and reading
- Productive: Speaking, writing and creating

General capabilities

- Literacy
- Information and communication technology capability
- Critical and creative thinking

Curriculum content in this unit

- Language for interaction: ACELA1541
- Text structure and organisation: ACELA1809, ACELA1544
- Expressing and developing ideas: ACELA1546, ACELA1547
- Examining literature: ACELT1629, ACELT1630, ACELT1767
- Interacting with others: ACELY1730, ACELY1808, ACELY1731
- Interpreting, analysing, evaluating: ACELY1732, ACELY1734
- Creating texts: ACELY1736, ACELY1810, ACELY1738

Responding to texts

'Fit for success'

To the Editor

As the Principal of our city's finest Secondary College, I know that every parent wants their child to succeed in the world. For children to succeed, they need to do well academically and play sports. Scientific research has proven that students who participate in sports do better at their studies. All parents want healthy children.

Recent reports in the New Kingston Gazette about the lack of trophies in our school's cabinet have sparked outrage and controversy within the school's community. I want to set the record straight now, once and for all.

Our school finished last in the basketball competition because we lost every single match. The one game our soccer team won was handed to them because the opposition forfeited. This debate is not only about trophies in the school cabinet, we also need better sports teams because we need fitter students. I believe that if students play sport they will become smarter: how can we expect anything less for our youth?

Think about this: a recent survey has revealed that only 2% of our students represent the school in sports. 90% of the students who play basketball are also members of the soccer team. Our athletics team consists of only five members; all of them are members of the Williams family. Absenteeism from PE class is at an all-time high 40%; attendance at the last School Sports Day was a pathetic 55%.

Parents of New Kingston children, I implore you. This appalling record must now end! And here is how I plan to help you end it. I am making it compulsory for all students to attend 'Sports Club' which will be held at 8 am for 30 minutes every morning. Students will participate in a variety of exercises: stretching to remain supple, jogging for aerobic fitness and learning teamwork skills.

I know that all concerned parents will agree with me because fit and healthy students obtain better results. If you do not agree, however, email your comments to my secretary.

Principal Paul Putman, New Kingston Secondary College, *New Kingston Gazette*, 20 June 2013.

Understanding 'Fit for success'

Read **'Fit for success'**, and then answer the following questions. You may use a dictionary.

1   Who is Paul Putman?

....

2   What percentage of students represent the school in sports?

....

3   What decision has Paul Putman made?

....

....

....

4   Tick one box only to answer each of the following questions:

a   What word best describes the language style in Paul Putman's letter?

jargon ❑   formal ❑   informal ❑

b   What type of text is Paul Putman's letter?

information text ❑   persuasive text ❑   poem ❑

c   Who is the intended audience for the letter?

teachers ❑   students ❑   parents ❑

d   Which best describes the purpose of the letter?

to explain why the school is hopeless at sports ❑

to persuade parents that involvement in sports will make their children successful at school ❑

to inform parents that Sports Club is compulsory ❑

Grammar tools

Clauses

A clause is a group of words that contains a subject and a verb. It forms a part or the whole of a sentence. There are two types of clauses:

1 The main clause

A main clause can stand by itself as a complete sentence.

Example: **I was running late home from school.**

2 The subordinate clause

A subordinate clause cannot stand by itself but offers extra information or meaning to a main clause. Sentences can have more than one subordinate clause.

Example: **because I attended soccer training.**

Conjunctions join clauses together so that a sentence makes sense.

Conjunction	Purpose
and besides	To join similar points
because as since for	To show reason
but however	To show differences or contrast

1 Write your own subordinate clauses to create new, complete sentences with the following main clauses from Principal Paul Putman's letter to the editor.

a For children to succeed, they need to do well academically

....

b Our school finished last in the basketball competition

....

c The one game our soccer team won was handed to them

....

2 Write your own main clauses and attach them to the following subordinate clauses.

a Because I play basketball ....

b .... and I can touch my toes.

c .... but we still lost.

More persuasive language techniques

Persuasive texts present an argument to the reader or audience. The overall goal of persuasive writing is to persuade you **to agree** with its point of view on a topic or issue. Persuasive language is used in speeches, letters, opinion articles and cartoons.

In addition to using persuasive language techniques such as facts, exaggeration and generalisations (refer to Unit 4, p. 43), texts such as letters to the editor often use **emotive language** to present a point of view.

Emotive language includes strong language that promotes an emotional response from the reader.

Tone reflects the writer's attitude towards the subject, for example, humorous, confident, passionate, aggressive, authoritative.

1   Briefly summarise the point of view that Principal Paul Putman is presenting in his letter.

....

....

....

2   Quote the two generalisations used by Principal Paul Putman in the first paragraph of his letter.

....

....

....

3 Quote the two facts in paragraph three of the letter.

_____

_____

4 Quote the examples of strong language in paragraph five of the letter that mean the following:

'ask' _____

'poor' _____

5 Describe Principal Paul Putman's tone.

_____

_____

_____

_____

_____

_____

_____

Spelling tools

Letters that sound like 'f'

Many words in the English language contain a combination of letters that make the same sound as the letter 'f'.

There are **three rules** to follow to make sure that both your pronunciation and spelling are correct:

1 'ph' sounds like 'f'

- start of words: physics, physical, phone, philosophy, physicist

- middle of words: nephew, hyphen, hemisphere, prophet, siphon, typhoon

- end of words: catastrophe, graph, epitaph, apostrophe

2 'gh' often sounds like 'f' if it follows the vowels 'ou'

- tough, cough, rough, trough, enough

However, it can also be silent, e.g. though, dough, ought, through, plough

3 'gh' often sounds like 'f' if it follows the vowels 'au'

- laugh, draught, laughter

However, it can also be silent, e.g. taught, daughter, naughty

---

1 Use a dictionary to help you find the following words that start with 'ph'. Definitions have been provided to assist you.

a ph _____ _____ _____ _____ (noun) a ghost or apparition

b ph _____ _____ _____ _____ _____ _____ _____ (adjective) appearing attractive in photographs

c ph _____ _____ _____ (adjective) false

d ph _____ _____ _____ _____ (noun) the study of the natural laws and properties of matter and energy

---

2 Underline the spelling mistakes in the following text and rewrite the words correctly in the space provided.

To Principal Putman

Don't make me laff! There is no way that I'm going to your tuff Sports Club. I don't do any ruff stuff. I have never attended fisical education classes because I have a coff and sometimes bring up flem. It would be a fenomenal catastrofe for the school if you make me play sports. I can't frow a ball or shoot baskets. It's fisically impossible for me to swim too!

Don Badman (fony name)

Punctuation tools

Colons and semicolons

Colons (:) are used in lead-in lines when you write bullet point lists (see Unit 12, p. 159). You also use colons to join two parts of a sentence.

Example: Paul has a few issues with his students: he thinks they are lazy and unfit.

In this example, the first part of the sentence contains the idea. The part that follows the colon provides an elaboration or explanation of the first part, or the reason why Paul has a few issues with his students.

Colons can also introduce lists of objects in a sentence, or lists of ideas.

Example: The following sports will be introduced at school: hockey, rugby, tennis and gymnastics.

Semicolons (;) link complete sentences and join ideas about the same topic or subject.

There are three rules you should follow when using semicolons:

1 They separate main clauses in sentences when the conjunctions 'and', 'but', 'for', 'or', 'consequently', 'therefore' or 'however' are omitted.

Example: Mia is an athlete; she loves to play basketball.

2 They separate items in a long list where commas are also used.

Example: The staff love sport, including tennis; water sports – like swimming and water polo; all snow sports and cycling.

3 They separate main clauses that are long and contain commas.

Example: Staff are disappointed that students are lazy, disinterested and undisciplined; that they are not interested in any sports and wag sports days.

1 Quote a sentence from paragraph four of the letter that uses semicolons.

2 Which of the semicolon rules are used in the sentence in question 1?

3 Rewrite the final paragraph of the letter using semicolons instead of conjunctions.

✂ Writing and creating tools

Writing task

Imagine you are a student at New Kingston Secondary College for whom it is now compulsory to attend Sports Club. Write a formal letter to the editor of your local newspaper expressing your point of view on why the Sports Club is not a good idea. Your letter will disagree with Principal Putman's letter and provide two reasons for this. You need to use persuasive language techniques, including emotive language. Your letter should be 200 words.

1 **Research** – What is Principal Putman's main argument? Consider how you will respond to the following points:

- reasons why some students don't want to play sports

- other schools' policies about sports participation

- reasons why students cannot attend 8 am sports sessions

- other ways to encourage students to play sports.

2 **Plan** – Think about the emotive language you will use to respond to each of the above points.

3 **Draft** – Write sentences in your own workbook under the following paragraph headings:

   a your opinion about the Sports Club being compulsory

   b the first reason why it should not be compulsory

   c the second reason why it should not be compulsory

   d your suggestions for ways in which students can be encouraged to play more sports.

4 **Edit and proofread** – Read over your letter. Has it followed the correct style and tone for a letter to the editor? Have you used persuasive language techniques? Check spelling and punctuation. Have you appealed to the emotions of your reader?

Creating task

Explore **multimodal presentation methods** for your persuasive letter.

- Take the major points from your letter and turn it into a PowerPoint presentation that combines visual texts such as photos and diagrams to help explain the main points of your argument.

- If you have access to a **digital video camera** or **video function** on your digital camera, obtain permission and make a short video about your school. Conduct mock interviews about the proposed compulsory Sports Club to find out what the student population thinks.

Listen and respond to what other students have done.

- Read your letter aloud as an **oral presentation** to your class.

- Survey your class after you read your letter. Ask them to identify your use of persuasive language techniques. Did these techniques persuade them to think differently about the issue? If so, why?

- Identify the different techniques used in your classmates' letters. Comment on which techniques you think were the most effective and why.

Unit  14

Literary texts: Personal memoir

Tools in this unit

- Reading tools: Understanding *Wonder*
- Grammar tools: Phrases and prepositions
- Vocabulary tools: Latin word origins
- Spelling tools: Suffixes for words ending in 'c'
- Punctuation tools: Compiling a bibliography
- Writing and creating tools: Write your own personal memoir

Modes covered

- Receptive: Reading, listening and viewing
- Productive: Speaking, writing and creating

General capabilities

- Literacy
- Personal and social capability
- Information and communication technology capability
- Critical and creative thinking
- Ethical understanding

Curriculum content in this unit

- Language for interaction: ACELA1541
- Text structure and organisation: ACELA1766, ACELA1809, ACELA1544
- Expressing and developing ideas: ACELA1547
- Literature and context: ACELT1626
- Responding to literature: ACELT1627, ACELT1807
- Examining literature: ACELT1629, ACELT1767
- Creating literature: ACELT1768
- Interacting with others: ACELY1808, ACELY1731
- Interpreting, analysing, evaluating: ACELY1732, ACELY1733, ACELY1735
- Creating texts: ACELY1736, ACELY1810, ACELY1738

Responding to texts

Wonder by R.J. Palacio (2012)

My name is August, by the way. I won't describe what I look like. Whatever you're thinking, it's probably worse... (p. 3)

Mum says by then they had told her all about me. She had been preparing herself for the seeing of me. But she says that when she looked down into my tiny mushed-up face for the first time, all she could see was how pretty my eyes were. (p. 7)

I hate the way I eat. I know how weird it looks. I had a surgery to fix my cleft palate when I was a baby, and then a second cleft surgery when I was four, but I still have a hole in the roof of my mouth. And even though I had jaw alignment surgery a few years ago, I have to chew food in the front of my mouth. .. I eat like a tortoise, if you've ever seen a tortoise eating. Like some prehistoric swamp thing. (p. 50)

I think it's like the Cheese Touch in *Diary of a Wimpy Kid*. The kids in the story were afraid they'd catch cooties if they touched the moldy old cheese on the basketball court. At Beecher Prep, I'm the moldy old cheese... (p. 72)

For me, Halloween is the best holiday in the world. It even beats Christmas. I get to dress up in a costume. I get to wear a mask. I get to go around like every other kid with a mask and nobody thinks I look weird. Nobody takes a second look. Nobody notices me. Nobody knows me... (p. 73)

Source: Palacio, R.J., 2003, *Wonder*, Random House Children's Books, London.

Understanding *Wonder*

Read the five separate extracts from **Wonder**, then answer the following questions. You may use a dictionary.

1   What is the narrator's name? _____

2a What does he eat like? _____

b   Why? Provide a quote to support your response. _____

_____

3   From what story does 'Cheese Touch' originate?

_____

4   List three reasons from the extracts that demonstrate that the narrator does not look like most other kids.

_____

_____

_____

5   Tick one box only to answer each of the following:

a   What is 'Beecher Prep'?

a novel ❑   a hospital ❑   a school ❑

b   The narrator sounds:

scared ❑   funny ❑   honest ❑

c   Which best describes the purpose of this extract?

to recall and describe events from childhood ❑

to persuade readers to play Cheese Touch ❑

to inform readers about Halloween ❑

Grammar tools

Phrases and prepositions

A **phrase** is a group of words without a verb that helps you to add information to a sentence. Phrases can be added at the beginning, middle or end of sentences.

Phrases often begin with **prepositions** and these are called **prepositional phrase**s – e.g. 'over the hill'. A preposition connects nouns and pronouns to other words and helps to tell us where things are. There are three main types of prepositions:

1 Prepositions that describe location

beside	between	above	below	under	on	in	over
near	inside	within	without	at	across	around	

Example: John walked under the bridge.

under is a preposition; under the bridge is a prepositional phrase.

2 Prepositions that describe time

after	before	during	at	past	until

Example: John talked during the movie.

during is a preposition; during the movie is a prepositional phrase.

3 Prepositions that describe a reason

as	by	without	to	for	since

Example: John is not at school since he is ill.

since is a preposition; since he is ill is a prepositional phrase.

1 Answer the following questions using phrases from the extract. Remember that they need to begin with a preposition.

a When did his mother think he had beautiful eyes? _____

b Where does he have a hole? _____

c In which story is the 'Cheese Touch' introduced?

_____

d Where is the moldy cheese? _____

e How does he walk around during Halloween?

_____

2 These sentences are missing prepositions and/or prepositional phrases. Add appropriate prepositions and/or prepositional phrases to make them complete. Preposition types are indicated in brackets.

a _____ Ahmed played a game _____ .
(time/location)

b Toni carefully hid her wallet _____ . (location)

c _____ the dog walked. (time)

d The boy held his arms up _____ . (reason)

e _____ the witch got her broomstick

_____ . (time/location)

f Ms Gonzo _____ told her students that she would be absent tomorrow

_____ . (time/reason)

g _____ Ms Gonzo left the class, the students clapped. (time)

h 'Walk _____ the road then go _____ until you

cross the river. Turn left and walk _____ for 3km. (location/location/

location)

i 'I've got detention _____ 5 o'clock,' complained the student. (time)

j _____ footy practice I have to race _____ to

the hall _____ meet mum for parent-teacher

interviews. (time/location/reason)

Vocabulary tools

Latin word origins

Many words in the English language come from Latin words.

Example: the word 'century' comes from **centum**, the Latin word for 'one hundred'.

Below are some other common Latin words and their English equivalents.

Latin word	Meaning	English word
annus	year	annual
liber	book	library
videre	to see	visual

1 Complete the following table by adding the English words from the list.

pupil   popular   pedestrian   vacuum   ingenious

hospitality   solar   gladiator   primitive

Latin word	Meaning	English word
manus	hand	manual
hospes	guest	
pupa	child	
ingenium	skill or talent	
primus	first	
vacuus	empty	
populus	the people	
sol	sun	
gladius	sword	
pes	foot	

2 Write definitions for the following Latin terms. You may use a dictionary.

a bona fide _____

b ad nauseam _____

c ego _____

d post mortem _____

_____

e carpe diem _____

f circa _____

g terra nova _____

⚒ Spelling tools ✎

Suffixes for words ending in 'c'

When adding a suffix to words that end in the letter 'c', you must follow these two rules:

1 If a word ends in 'c', add a 'k' before adding the suffixes 'ed', 'ing', 'er' and 'y'.

Example: picnic + ing = picnicking

2 If adding any other suffixes to words that end in 'c', do not add a 'k'.

Example: arithmetic + ally = arithmetically

1 Rewrite the following words adding the suffixes in the brackets.

a traffic (ing) _____   **b** optic (al) _____

c static (ally) _____   **d** mimic (ed) _____

e panic (ing) _____   **f** frolic (some) _____

2 Underline the 10 spelling mistakes in the text below and write the words correctly in the space provided.

Family picnic

Once, when I was four years old, our entire family picniced in the park. There were 10 of us plus our dog so it was statistickally impossible for us to fit into one car. Mum, who was optickally challenged, paniced because she had to drive Nana, two kids, the baby and the dog. Nana mimiced her favourite cartoon character the whole journey while the colicy baby cried non-stop.

At the park we discovered that we had only brought one of the three boxes of food. Arithmetickally, that meant half a sausage and a quarter of a lamington each. Our frolicksome dog bit other picnicers and stole their food. Somehow Nana ended up with another family singing classickal tunes. We bought fish and chips on the way home.

_____

_____

_____

_____

_____

_____

_____

Punctuation tools

Compiling a bibliography

A bibliography is a detailed alphabetical list of books, newspaper and magazine articles, films and websites – i.e. all the references – that you use to gather information for your projects and essays. The bibliography usually appears at the end of your project or essay.

A bibliography is important because:

- it provides a clear record of your sources and allows your teacher to see the kind of research you have done prior to writing

- it shows that you have not copied or plagiarised your ideas but have acknowledged the resources that have helped to shape them.

There are different styles of bibliographies, but all use alphabetical lists. The Harvard Author-Date system is one of the most commonly used and follows the format below, beginning with the author's surname:

Six components of the Harvard style of bibliography:

1 Author's surname followed by a comma

2 Initial of author's first name

3 Year of publication followed by a comma

4 Title in *italics* (quotation marks are acceptable if you are writing by hand) followed by a comma

5 Publisher's name followed by a comma

6 Place of publication followed by a full stop.

Example: Hayes, A 2014, *Language Toolkit 2*, Cambridge University Press, Melbourne.

Fix it!

Plagiarism is referring to another author's words or ideas without acknowledging them. It is important to include an acknowledgement every time you refer to or directly quote another author's words or ideas, to avoid accusations of plagiarism or cheating.

1 Refer to the previous rules and rewrite the following as entries in a Harvard-style bibliography.

a *When I Was a Boy*, Davis J Australia 2002 Random House

....

b H 2009 Penguin Books, Australia, *Surf's Up!* Lucas

....

c Pankhurst, Australia, *Women's Work*, Black Dog Books, D 2010

....

2 Research and write three entries for a bibliography on one of the topics below.

healthy   food   tennis   volcanoes   Elvis Presley   Confucius

....

....

....

....

....

....

Writing and creating tools

Writing task

Find a photo of yourself when you were about seven or eight years of age. Write a description of yourself and what you are doing in the photo. Use lots of phrases and prepositions to describe your memories of the time when this photo was taken. In your description, consider also how it feels to look back and think about the past. Your personal memoir should be 250 words.

1 **Research** – Use a thesaurus to help you find a wide variety of adjectives and verbs to describe the photo. Write notes to answer the following questions:

- What are you doing in the photo?

- What are you wearing?

- Is there anyone else in the photo?

- Who are they?

- Do you remember what happened before and after this photo was taken?

- What did people say to you?

- What did you say to them?

- What were you thinking?

2 **Plan** – Number your points in the order that you want them to appear in your memoir.

3 **Draft** – Write your memoir. Work on your prepositions and phrases. Give your memoir a title that describes the events you are recounting.

4 **Edit and proofread** – Read over your piece. Have you included interesting phrases? Check your spelling and punctuation.

Creating task

Explore **multimodal presentation methods** for your personal memoir.

- If you have access to the free downloadable software program Microsoft Photo Story 3, use it to turn this memory into a **digital story** with text and images. Locate other photos of yourself from this time and put them together to tell another story about yourself.

Listen and respond to what other students have done.

- Read your personal memoir to the class as an **oral presentation**.

- **Reflect on** the language choices made by your classmates. In small groups make lists of the different adjectives used in the memoirs.

- Rank the best 10 adjectives from one to 10. Do you think your classmates chose the best adjectives to describe their experiences?

Unit  15

Literary texts: Narrative voice

Tools in this unit

- Reading tools: Understanding *A Bridge to Wiseman's Cove*
- Grammar tools: Subject and verb agreement
- Vocabulary tools: Active and passive voice
- Spelling tools: Silent letters in the middle of a word – 't', 'd'
- Punctuation tools: Dashes
- Writing and creating tools: Write a short fiction piece in the active voice

Modes covered

- Receptive: Reading, listening and viewing
- Productive: Speaking, writing and creating

General capabilities

- Literacy
- Information and communication technology capability
- Critical and creative thinking

Curriculum content in this unit

- Text structure and organisation: ACELA1766, ACELA1809
- Literature and context: ACELT1626
- Responding to literature: ACELT1627, ACELT1807
- Examining literature: ACELT1629, ACELT1767
- Interacting with others: ACELY1808, ACELY1731
- Interpreting, analysing, evaluating: ACELY1732, ACELY1733, ACELY1735
- Creating texts: ACELY1736, ACELY1810, ACELY1738

Responding to texts

A *Bridge to Wiseman's Cove* by James Maloney (1996)

When Carl was four years old, his mother lost him at the shopping mall. The faces still haunted his sleep. A kindly man calmed his terror, dried his tears with a musty handkerchief and held his hand as they walked to the Information desk. The woman there hugged him and sat him on the counter cooing, 'Mummy won't be long. She's looking for you,' sounding less convinced as each hour passed. Then the police and the questions and the disapproval and the ride home in the police car to find Kerry dry-eyed and unrepentant. 'I'm on my own,' she shouted at the coppers. Only after the police had left did she begin to cry.

Years later, Kerry lost herself. Just didn't come home from the supermarket. Sarah cooked tea, bathed Harley, dressed him and put him to bed. Did the same the next night and the next, while Carl watched and helped where he could. Their mother came back on the fourth day. Ashamed. Desperate.

Harley clung to her. Sarah screamed and raged. Carl stood back, watching.

This happened again a year later, then a third time, until Carl came to know the signs and could almost predict his mother's escape. There was a frantic mood, the screeching, the recrimination. What are you doing here? You're mucking up my life. I can't stand it.

Source: Maloney, J. 1996, *A Bridge to Wiseman's Cove*, University of Queensland Press, Brisbane, p. 4.

Understanding A Bridge to Wiseman's Cove

Read the extract from **A Bridge to Wiseman's Cove**, then answer the following questions. You may use a dictionary.

1 Who are the four members of the family mentioned in the extract? ....

....

2 Who is Kerry? ....

3 Who found Carl when he was lost? ....

....

4 What was Sarah's reaction towards Kerry when she returned? Why? ....

....

....

....

5 Write definitions for the following words:

a unrepentant ....

....

b recrimination ....

....

6 Tick one box only to answer each of the following questions:

a Which best describes the type of text this extract comes from?

a letter ☐   a novel ☐   a poem ☐

---

b Which best describes the character of the mother?

lazy ☐ incapable ☐ cruel ☐

Subject and verb agreement

For a sentence to be grammatically correct, the subject and verb must always agree in number (singular or plural) and person. To find the subject of a sentence you ask, 'Who or what performs the verb?'

Example: **The boy hides** from his mother. Verb = hides

Who or what hides? Subject = the boy

Singular subjects (one)	I you she he the dog everyone anyone each no one nobody
Plural subjects (more than one)	we our they the teams five dogs the mum and her children Sarah and Harley

Fix it!

'Everyone', 'each', 'none' and 'nobody' are all singular subjects and must be followed by singular verbs. For example: Nobody does homework on Friday nights.

1 Identify the verb and subject in each of the following sentences and write them in the spaces provided.

a Sarah washed Harley.

Verb _____ Subject _____

b Mother returned on the fourth day.

Verb _____ Subject _____

c Kerry lost Carl at the supermarket.

Verb _____ Subject _____

d A kindly man dried his tears.

Verb _____ Subject _____

2 Add the correct verb to the following sentences.

a Everyone _____ TV in the evenings. (watch/watches)

b 'I am _____ to run a marathon soon!' exclaimed Cliff. (plans/planning)

c Three black cats _____ on the fence under a full moon. (sat/sats)

d Stephen and Suresh _____ in the same team. (were/was)

e Each of the students _____ their own calculator. (has/have)

f Anyone can _____ French if they try. (speak/speaks)

g The teams _____ places every hour. (change/changes)

h We tested our product and 10 cats _____ that 'Go cat' tinned food is the best. (agrees/agree)

i My parents _____ me to be a doctor when I finish school. (wants/want)

Active and passive voice

Sentences are constructed in either the **active** or the **passive** voice. Whether the voice is active or passive is dependent on how the verb is used.

Active voice

When the subject performs or does the action, the verb is active.

Example: Sarah cooked the dinner.

verb = cooked   who cooked = **subject** = Sarah did

The active voice makes a text more immediate, interesting and personal, and is often used in the writing of **first-person narratives** (see Unit 8).

Passive voice

When the subject of the sentence receives the action, the verb is passive.

Example: The dinner was cooked by Sarah.

The passive voice is useful when writing reports, as it produces a more impersonal and objective style of writing.

1   Rewrite the following sentences using the active voice.

a   Carl's tears were dried by a kindly man.

----

b   Harley was bathed by Sarah.

----

c Harley was held by his sister.

----

d He was driven home by the police.

----

2 Rewrite the following sentences using the passive voice.

a Grace yelled at Simon.

----

b The cat coughed up a fur ball.

----

c Lulu forgot her house key.

----

d Jane lied to her teacher.

Spelling tools

Silent letters in the middle of a word – 't', 'd'

There are many words that contain letters that are not pronounced. These are known as silent letters. Many words have a silent 't' and 'd' located in the middle – you should watch out for these letters when spelling these words.

Rules for silent 't' and 'd' in the middle of words

1 When there is a three-letter combination of 'tch' in the middle of the word, the 't' is always silent.

Examples: watcher, kitchen, hatchet, satchel, stretcher, butcher, switcher

2 When you have the three-letter combination of 'dge' in the middle of a word, the 'd' is always silent and the combination is pronounced 'j'.

Examples: judged, lodger, codger, wedged, badger, gadget, dodger

1 Underline the spelling mistakes in the following sentences and write the correct spellings in the spaces provided.

a The student's sachel sat on the table. _____

b The juge instructed the jury to listen to the evidence carefully. _____

c The loger was evicted when he failed to pay his rent. _____

d In the kichen, the children made grilled cheese sandwiches and watched TV.

_____

2 Complete the text below using words from the box. Hints are in brackets.

hatchet   judged   badger   gadget   watcher   wedged

Forest tale

In the forest, the (animal) _____ was running from the hunter

who carried a sharp (tool) _____. It somehow got itself (trapped)

_____ between a rock and a tree and could not escape.

A (person) _____ witnessed the scene from his position up a tree and (decided) _____ that the animal needed his help. He used a special (device) _____ to free the animal and the hunter missed out!

🛠 Punctuation tools

Dashes

Dashes (–) are different from hyphens (see Unit 3, p. 35). A dash is used for the following purposes:

1 To add extra information to a sentence.

Example: Alex bought lunch – hot chips, of course – and everyone was happy.

2 To indicate a break in the sentence or highlight words or phrases at the end of a sentence.

Example: 'I was just stung by a bee – boy it hurts!'

3 To link information in a sentence.

Example: Alex went to Jim's house three times – Monday, Tuesday and Friday.

4 To indicate a deliberate omission of letters or a word (e.g. to imply swearing).

Example: 'I hate b— bees!'

1 Rewrite the following sentences adding dashes where necessary. You may need to cross out some words.

a 'Any student who misses the test for whatever reason will sit a make-up test!'

b 'Harley is an unhappy boy a very difficult, sad and lonely boy.

c 'There will be a test on Thursday and Friday next week,' said Ms Finch.

d I don't know what else to say but sorry.

e Sarah was on her way home via the corner store and would see Harley soon.

Writing and creating tools

Writing task

Choose a topic from the box below and write a 250-word short fiction piece narrated in the first person using the active voice. Be sure that there is agreement between subjects and verbs in your sentences. Use dashes to make your sentences more interesting. Your story needs to be imaginative and does not have to be based on something that happened to you. (Refer to Unit 8, Narrative conventions, p. 101.)

| lost at the zoo | a picnic in the park | driving home during a thunderstorm |
| baking a cake | running a marathon | shopping for Christmas |

1 **Research** – Choose a topic. Revise information on the active and the passive voice. Write notes on what your story will be about. Who will the narrator of your story be? How old are they? How do they sound when they speak? What language will they use?

2 **Plan** – Decide the order in which you want the information in your short story to be revealed.

3 **Draft** – Write your draft, including sentences with dashes.

4 **Edit and proofread** – It is very important that you read over your story. Is the voice of the narrator active or passive? If it is not active, now is the time to revise and edit your sentences to be sure they are not written in the passive voice. Check your spelling and punctuation.

Creating task

Explore **multimodal presentation methods** for your short fiction piece.

- Rewrite your short fiction piece in the passive voice. Make an audio recording of your original short fiction and of the new version in the passive voice. Broadcast your stories as a **podcast**.

Listen and respond to what other students have done.

- Read your short fiction piece to the class as an **oral presentation**. Read both the active voice and the passive voice versions.

- Ask your classmates to comment on which version is easier to understand and which version is more engaging for the audience. What difference does writing in the active and the passive voice make to your overall understanding of the story?

- Swap stories with your classmates. Change the order of events – move the end to the beginning, the middle to the end, etc. What impact does this have on the meaning of the narrative? Does this make the story more or less interesting for the reader?

Unit 16

Understanding Shakespeare

Tools in this unit

- Reading tools: Understanding *Much Ado about Nothing*
- Grammar tools: Articles
- Vocabulary tools: Shakespeare's language
- Spelling tools: Shakespeare spelling list
- Punctuation tools: Dramatic style
- Writing and creating tools: Write a drama script

Modes covered

- Receptive: Reading, listening and viewing
- Productive: Speaking, writing and creating

General capabilities

- Literacy
- Information and communication technology capability
- Critical and creative thinking

Curriculum content in this unit

- Language for interaction: ACELA1542
- Text structure and organisation: ACELA1766, ACELA1809, ACELA1544
- Expressing and developing ideas: ACELA1549, ACELA1547, ACELA1549
- Responding to literature: ACELT1627
- Examining literature: ACELT1629, ACELT1630, ACELT1767
- Creating literature: ACELT1632, ACELT1768
- Texts in context: ACELY1729
- Interacting with others: ACELY1808, ACELY1731
- Interpreting, analysing, evaluating: ACELY1732, ACELY1733, ACELY1734
- Creating texts: ACELY1736, ACELY1810, ACELY1738

Responding to texts

Much Ado about Nothing by William Shakespeare

William Shakespeare's language was the language of the time, and was designed to entertain audiences with lots of colourful insults and jokes. He often used lists in his comedies.

In his comedy, *Much Ado About Nothing*, Benedick tells the Prince Don Pedro, his commander, all the things he would rather do than meet Beatrice.

Enter CLAUDIO and BEATRICE, LEONATO and HERO

DON PEDRO   Look, here she comes.

BENEDICK   Will your grace command me any service to the world's end? I will go on the slightest errand now to the Antipodes that you can devise to send me on: I will fetch you a tooth-picker now from the furthest inch of Asia: bring you the length of Prester John's foot: fetch you a hair off the Great Cham's beard: do you embassage to the Pygmies, rather than hold three words conference with this Harpy: you have no employment for me?

Act 2, Scene 1, lines 198–205

Shakespeare mocks the making of lists through Dogberry, the foolish constable in *Much Ado About Nothing*, who lists his complaints against the men he has arrested.

DON PEDRO   Officers, what offence have these men done?

DOGBERRY   Marry, sit, they have committed false report, moreover they have spoken untruths, secondarily, they are slanders, sixth and lastly, they have belied a lady, thirdly they have verified unjust things, and to conclude, they are lying knaves.

Act 5, Scene 1, lines 190–194

Understanding *Much Ado About Nothing*

Read both extracts from ***Much Ado About Nothing***, then answer the following questions. You may need to do some extra research.

1   In the first extract, list the five things Benedick would rather do than meet Beatrice.

....

....

....

....

2   Match the key terms from Benedick's list to their explanations.

Harpy   Prester John   Antipodes   Great Cham   embassage

a   an errand ....

b   opposite side of the earth ....

c   emperor of the Mongols ....

d   birdlike monster with a beautiful female face ....

e   legendary Christian king in Africa or Asia ....

3   Who were 'groundlings'? ....

....

4   What were the silly/crazy characters known as?

....

....

5 List the three types of plays Shakespeare wrote. ....

....

6 In the second extract, quote the six different ways Dogberry has accused his prisoners of lying.

....

....

....

....

....

....

7 Who is Don Pedro?

....

8 Complete these famous quotes from Shakespeare's plays. You will need to do some research and you may use the internet. Complete the quote and identify the play.

a 'All the world's a ....' ....

b ' .... , ... ! wherefore art thou

.... ?'

c 'My kingdom for a ....' ....

d 'Double, double, toil and ....' ....

e ' .... , perchance to dream.' ....

f 'The course of .... never did run

smooth.' ....

g 'All that glisters ....'

....

Grammar tools

Articles

In the English language, there are three articles: **a**, **an**, and **the**.

These three articles are seperated into two types:

1 Definite

Definite article 'the' refers to a particular item or items.

Example: Police arrested **the** thief who broke into the theatre.

This means that police arrested the particular thief who broke into the theatre.

2 Indefinite

Indefinite articles 'a' and 'an' do not refer to particular items.

Example: Police arrested a thief.

This means that police arrested a thief, not the particular thief who broke into the theatre.

Note this:

'a' is used when the next word begins with a consonant. *Example:* a stage

'an' is used when the next word begins with a vowel. *Example:* an actor

1 In the following extract from Tony Thompson's book, *Shakespeare: The Most Famous Man in London* (2009), identify the **nine articles** he uses and write them in the space below.

The Globe opened on 12 June 1599 with a performance of *Julius Caesar*. William Shakespeare must have been inspired by the new venue. His next few plays are among his finest. It is at the Globe that he began to dig deep into his characters and grapple with complex philosophical problems. *Hamlet* followed in the same year, and with the famous 'to be or not to be' line, remains one of Shakespeare's most important works. It explores philosophical questions that continue to challenge audiences. It also contains numerous references to acting, actors and theatres. Shakespeare uses the visit of a travelling theatre company to Hamlet's castle at Elsinore to comment on the state of London theatre. Rival theatre companies are one of his targets. (p. 102)

....

....

....

2 Following the rules above, add the correct indefinite article to these words.

a .... audience   **b** .... director

c .... critic   **d** .... costume

e .... opening   **f** .... idea

3 Complete the following by adding the correct articles, definite and indefinite.

a I saw _____ actor near _____ stage.

_____ actor was very tall.

b _____ only copy of _____ script was locked in

_____ box.

c _____ audience at _____ Globe had to pay to

watch _____ play.

d Shakespeare was _____ great playwright. He was probably

_____ greatest playwright in Elizabethan times.

Vocabulary tools

Shakespeare's language

When you first read one of Shakespeare's plays, the words he uses may not immediately make sense to you. Even the insults he used are different from the ones we use to insult each other today!

A dictionary probably won't be helpful, as many of the words used in Shakespeare's time are now obsolete (no longer in use).

Examples:

thou has been replaced by **you**

thine has been replaced by **your**

wherefore has been replaced by **why**

art has been replaced by **are**

hath has been replaced by **has**

As with poetry, it helps to read Shakespeare's language aloud. After all, it was written to be performed. The following tips will also help you to make sense of Shakespeare's language throughout your school years:

1 Think or guess about how the word or phrase is used.

2 Read the surrounding words and stage directions to understand the context.

3 Look for clues.

1 Below is a brief section of dialogue from one of Shakespeare's comedies, *A Midsummer Night's Dream*. Some of the phrases have been highlighted. Read the extract aloud and then write what you think the highlighted phrases mean in the space provided.

DEMETRIUS **I love thee not**, therefore pursue me not.

Where is Lysander, and **fair** Hermia?

The one I'll slay, the other slayeth me.

Thou told'st me they were **stol'n** unto this wood,

And here am I, and wood within this wood

Because I cannot meet my Hermia.

Hence, **get thee gone**, and follow me no more.

HELENA   You **draw** me, you hard-hearted adamant!

But yet you draw not iron, for my heart

Is true as steel. Leave your power to draw,

And I shall have no power to follow you.

Act 2, Scene 1, lines 188–98

-----

2 Referring to what you learned in Unit 9 (p. 115) about **similes** and **metaphors**, can you identify the **metaphor** in the dialogue above? Write it in the space below. What do you think it means?

Shakespeare spelling list

Some words or dramatic terms recur frequently throughout Shakespeare's plays. You should learn what they mean and practise spelling them.

Acts	Divisions of plays; plays were divided into five acts, which were further divided into scenes
Aside	A brief comment made by a character to the audience that other characters cannot hear
Chorus	Group of people who introduce the play
Fool	A character who seems foolish but is actually very wise and makes comments about other characters
Ghosts	Murdered people who come back to haunt their killers
Noble persons	High-status citizens, wealthy and usually loyal to the king, although they sometimes betray him
Prologue	The introduction at the start of a play
Soliloquy	A speech by one character that reveals their inner thoughts
Soothsayer	Someone who predicts the future
The Globe Theatre	The outdoor theatre where Shakespeare's plays were performed
Witches	Supernatural characters who speak in riddles

1 Underline the eleven spelling mistakes in the following email and write the correct versions in the space below.

Hi Cordelia

Not sure if I can help with your assignment about Shakespeare but here goes. His plays had gosts and wiches in them. (I would like my own soofsayer to predict useful stuff like who will win the

World Cup.) He also had wealthy nobil people in his plays who sometimes betrayed the kings and queens and then got killed.

There's a guy called a Fule who is secretly smart. When a guy on stage tells his thoughts to the audience it's called a solilokway. An assyde is when they put their hand to their mouth and make a comment to the audience that other guys on stage can't hear (as if?)

His plays were performed at The Glob Theatre and sometimes there was a corus but I don't know what they do. A prolog can introduce (or was it end?) a play. Plays had 5 ax. I think his first name was William or Romeo. Not sure.

L8R, Dragan :-)

Dramatic style

Shakespeare's plays were written in script format. This is the standard format for a play and the presentation of dramatic dialogue. When you write a scene for a play you must set it out in this way. A playscript includes the following:

- character names to indicate who speaks
- stage directions (instructions for actors and directors)
- lines for dialogue
- scene title
- act number and scene number
- line number.

Read and examine the following extract from Shakespeare's most popular tragedy, *Romeo and Juliet*, then answer the questions about dramatic style.

The Great Hall in Capulet's Mansion

Enter	[CAPULET, LADY CAPULET, JULIET, TYBALT *and his* PAGE, NURSE, *and all the* GUESTS *and* GENTLEWOMEN *to the* Maskers.]
CAPULET	Welcome, gentlemen! Ladies that have their toes
	Unplagued with corns will walk a bout with you.
	Ah, my mistresses, which of you all
	Will now deny to dance? She that makes dainty,
	She I'll swear hath corns. Am I come near ye now?
	Welcome, gentlemen! I have seen the day
	That I have worn a visor and could tell
	A whispering tale in a fair lady's ear,
	Such as would please; 'tis gone, 'tis gone, 'tis gone.
	You are welcome, gentlemen. Come, musicians, play.

Music plays

> A hall, a hall, give room! and foot it, girls.

And they dance.

> More light, you knaves, and turn the tables up;
>
> . . .

COUSIN CAPULET   Berlady, thirty years.

Act 1, Scene 5, lines 15–33

1   Where and how do you write the names of the characters who speak?

_____

_____

2   How do you show when a new character is speaking?

_____

_____

3   Who are stage directions written for? Write down one of the stage directions from the extract above.

_____

_____

4   Where do you write the location or setting of the scene?

_____

_____

5   Are quotation marks used for dialogue? _____

Writing and creating tools

Writing task

Use the format for writing a script to write your own short scene – 250 words – between two to three characters on one of the following topics. Do not use Shakespearean language.

going to the movies	countdown to the big game	first date
preparing for a birthday party	the day before Christmas	an argument

1 **Research** – Choose your topic. Decide how many characters you will include. What do they want? How will they sound? How old are they?

2 **Plan** – Work out who will speak first and how the other characters will respond. In what order will they speak and how many times?

3 **Draft** – Write a draft of your script.

4 **Edit and proofread** – Check that you have used the correct format for dramatic language. Have you used stage directions? Give your scene an act and scene number. Read the scene aloud.

Creating task

In small groups choose one of the finished scripts to perform. Or, if you have access to a **digital video camera**, record the performance. You might wish to broadcast the performance on **YouTube** – only after you have obtained permission from everyone first.

Listen and respond to what other students have done.

*   Either individually or in groups (depending on how many speaking parts there are in your script), read your script as an **oral presentation** to the class.

*   Describe the language used. Is it formal or informal? Does it communicate clearly what is happening in the scene? What does the language reveal about the characters?

Revision tools: Units 13–16

Complete these questions by yourself. You may use a dictionary.

Grammar tools

Family picnic

Nana stayed in her room on Sunday. She refused to attend a family picnic because she said that the family had abandoned her at the last picnic. Nana complained that the food made by Mum was 'rubbish' and that she had to sit in the back seat of Mum's car. Mum rolled her eyes. Nana could eat take-away food and sit in the front seat of his car was a suggestion made by Dad. A very large park with a deep pond was the picnic place suggested by Mum.

Read 'Family picnic', then answer the following questions.

1   Circle the verb and underline the subject in the following sentences.

a   Nana stayed in her room on Sunday.

b   Mum rolled her eyes.

2   Locate phrases to answer the following questions. Remember to include prepositions.

a   Where did Nana stay? ....

b   When had the family abandoned her? ....

c   Where did Nana have to sit? ....

d   What did the park also have? ....

3   Quote the subordinate clause in the third sentence of 'Family picnic'.

....

4   Quote the main clause in the second sentence of 'Family picnic'.

....

Vocabulary tools

5 Rewrite the last two sentences of 'Family picnic' in active form.

....

....

....

....

Spelling tools

6 Rewrite the following 'ph' words correctly:

a fisical ....

b fony ....

c epitaf ....

d fonetic ....

e profet ....

f grafic ....

7 Rewrite the following words adding the suffixes in the brackets.

a picnic (ing) ....

b traffic (ed) ....

c panic (ing) ....

d magic (ally) ....